The UK
Tefal Dual Easy Fry & Grill
Cookbook for Beginners

Easy & Tasty Tefal Recipes Make Your Meals a Breeze and Transform Kitchen Experience into a Culinary Adventure | Full-Colour Edition

Charlene Helsley

•Contents•

Introduction

The Tefal Dual Easy Fry & Grill is the ultimate kitchen companion for anyone looking to combine the convenience of air frying with the versatility of grilling, all in one compact device. This appliance allows you to enjoy healthier versions of your favourite meals without compromising on flavour or texture. Whether you are new to air frying or already an enthusiast, this cookbook is designed to help you make the most of your Tefal Dual Easy Fry & Grill.

With a focus on ease and practicality, the UK Tefal Dual Easy Fry & Grill Cookbook brings a diverse range of delicious recipes tailored to suit all tastes and occasions. From crispy chips and tender grilled meats to perfectly roasted vegetables and delectable desserts, this book covers everything from weekday dinners to weekend indulgences. Each recipe has been meticulously tested and adapted for the UK kitchen, ensuring you can enjoy the perfect balance of convenience, flavour, and nutrition.

For busy families, those with hectic schedules, or individuals keen to explore new cooking methods, this cookbook offers simple, easy-to-follow instructions and time-saving tips. Not only will you find ideas for traditional British favourites, but also a variety of global-inspired dishes that will transform your mealtime experience. Whether you're grilling succulent meats or air frying healthier alternatives, this book will guide you through every step, making the Tefal Dual Easy Fry & Grill an indispensable tool in your kitchen.

Embark on a culinary journey with this versatile appliance and discover how you can enjoy flavourful, nutritious meals with minimal effort.

Fundamentals of Tefal Dual Easy Fry & Grill

The Tefal Dual Easy Fry & Grill combines the functionality of air frying and grilling in one versatile appliance, making it an excellent addition to any kitchen. It offers a healthier way to cook your favourite dishes with little to no oil, delivering crispy and delicious results. This appliance boasts a digital touchscreen with eight pre-set programmes, ensuring effortless and precise cooking. Air frying and grilling are made simple and efficient.

With its large capacity, the Dual Easy Fry & Grill is ideal for families or meal preparation, while its sleek design fits neatly on any countertop. The removable, non-stick basket and grill plate are dishwasher safe, ensuring easy cleaning. It also features adjustable temperature control and a 60-minute timer, guaranteeing perfectly cooked meals every time.

Whether you're preparing chips, chicken, vegetables, or steaks, the Tefal Dual Easy Fry & Grill consistently delivers outstanding results. It's a perfect choice for those who want to enjoy healthier meals without compromising on taste or texture. With its innovative design and user-friendly features, this appliance makes cooking simpler and helps you create delicious, nutritious meals with ease.

What is Tefal Dual Easy Fry & Grill?

The Tefal Dual Easy Fry & Grill is a versatile kitchen appliance that combines the convenience of air frying with the precision of grilling in one sleek unit. Designed to help you cook healthier meals with ease, this innovative device offers a practical solution for those who love crispy fried foods but want to reduce their oil intake. It allows you to prepare delicious, golden meals with little to no oil, making it an ideal option for anyone looking to adopt a healthier lifestyle without compromising on taste or texture.

One of the standout features of the Tefal Dual Easy Fry & Grill is its dual functionality, which enables you to air fry and grill a wide variety of foods. The appliance comes with a digital touchscreen, offering eight pre-set programmes that allow you to cook different types of food at the touch of a button. Whether you're cooking chips, grilled vegetables, chicken, or even steaks, the Tefal Dual Easy Fry & Grill delivers consistent, evenly cooked results with minimal effort.

This appliance also features an adjustable temperature control, ensuring that you can achieve perfect results every time, regardless of the recipe. The 60-minute timer provides added convenience, allowing you to set your cooking time and walk away, knowing that the appliance will automatically stop once the time is up.

In addition to its impressive functionality, the Tefal Dual Easy Fry & Grill is designed with practicality in mind. Its large 4.2-litre capacity makes it perfect for families or for

those who like to prepare meals in advance. Despite its generous size, the appliance has a compact, sleek design that fits neatly on any countertop. The removable non-stick basket and grill plate are dishwasher-safe, making the cleaning process hassle-free.

The Tefal Dual Easy Fry & Grill is not just about convenience – it also encourages healthier cooking. By air frying instead of deep-frying, you can significantly reduce the amount of fat in your meals while still achieving that satisfying crunch. At the same time, the grill function allows you to cook meats, fish, and vegetables to perfection, ensuring even cooking without the need for excessive oil.

In conclusion, the Tefal Dual Easy Fry & Grill is a versatile, user-friendly appliance that simplifies the cooking process while promoting healthier eating habits. Its combination of air frying and grilling in one unit makes it a must-have for anyone looking to create delicious, nutritious meals with minimal effort.

Advantages of Using It

The Tefal Dual Easy Fry & Grill is an exceptional addition to any kitchen, designed to enhance your cooking experience while promoting a healthier lifestyle. Combining two highly effective cooking methods – air frying and grilling – this innovative appliance offers a range of benefits that make it a versatile, user-friendly choice. Below are 15 key benefits of using the Tefal Dual Easy Fry & Grill, demonstrating how it can revolutionise your kitchen routine.

1.Healthier Cooking

One of the most significant benefits of the Tefal Dual Easy Fry & Grill is its ability to help you prepare healthier meals. Air frying uses little to no oil, significantly reducing the fat content in your dishes. This makes it ideal for those who want to enjoy their favourite fried foods, such as chips and chicken wings, without the added guilt. By reducing oil consumption, the appliance also lowers your intake of calories and unhealthy fats, contributing to better overall health.

2.Crispy and Delicious Results

Despite the reduction in oil, the Tefal Dual Easy Fry & Grill still delivers the crispy texture and delicious taste that people love in fried foods. The hot air circulation technology ensures that your food is cooked evenly, achieving that golden-brown finish without the need for deep frying. Whether you're cooking chips, chicken, or fish, this appliance consistently produces satisfying results.

3.Dual Functionality

The combination of air frying and grilling in one appliance is a major advantage of the Tefal Dual Easy Fry & Grill. This dual functionality allows you to switch between or combine two cooking methods, giving you more flexibility in the kitchen. Whether you're air frying chips or grilling steaks, the Tefal Dual Easy Fry & Grill covers both bases, making it a highly versatile appliance for a wide range of dishes.

4.Energy Efficiency

Compared to traditional ovens, the Tefal Dual Easy Fry & Grill is far more energy-efficient. Its compact size and rapid heating capabilities mean it consumes less energy while delivering faster cooking times. You can save on electricity bills and reduce your environmental footprint without sacrificing the quality of your meals.

5.Large Capacity for Families

With a generous 4.2-litre capacity, the Tefal Dual Easy Fry & Grill is well-suited to families or those who enjoy meal prepping. Its spacious interior allows you to cook larger portions in one go, reducing the need for multiple batches. This is especially useful when preparing meals for family dinners, social gatherings, or bulk cooking for the week ahead.

6.Digital Touchscreen and Pre-Set Programmes

The appliance features a digital touchscreen with eight pre-set programmes, making cooking a breeze. These programmes are designed for specific foods, such as chips, chicken, fish, and vegetables, allowing you to cook them perfectly at the touch of a button. The intuitive interface makes it easy to navigate, even for those who are new to air frying and grilling.

7.Adjustable Temperature Control

For those who like to experiment with different recipes, the adjustable temperature control on the Tefal Dual Easy Fry & Grill is a valuable feature. You can manually set the temperature to suit the specific requirements of your dish, ensuring optimal cooking results every time. This flexibility allows you to cook everything from delicate fish to hearty steaks with precision.

8.60-Minute Timer

The built-in 60-minute timer is a practical feature that makes cooking more convenient. You can set the timer to match your recipe, and the appliance will automatically switch off when the cooking time is complete. This means you don't have to constantly monitor the cooking process, allowing you to multitask in the kitchen or focus on other activities while your food is being prepared.

9.Easy to Clean

Cleaning up after cooking is often the least enjoyable part of meal preparation, but the Tefal Dual Easy Fry & Grill makes it simple. The removable basket and grill plate are non-stick and dishwasher-safe, making the cleaning process quick and hassle-free. The non-stick surface ensures that food residue is easy to wipe away, reducing the time and effort spent scrubbing.

10.Compact and Stylish Design

The sleek, modern design of the Tefal Dual Easy Fry & Grill ensures that it fits seamlessly into any kitchen, regardless of size or decor. Its compact footprint takes up minimal counter space, making it ideal for small kitchens or those with limited storage. Despite its large capacity, the appliance is designed to be both stylish and functional, adding a touch of sophistication to your kitchen.

11.Even Cooking with Hot Air Circulation

The advanced hot air circulation technology used in the Tefal Dual Easy Fry & Grill ensures that your food is cooked evenly from all sides. This eliminates the need for constant turning or shaking, as the hot air circulates around the food to achieve consistent cooking results. Whether you're air frying chips or grilling chicken, you

can trust that your meal will be evenly cooked without any cold or undercooked spots.

12.Suitable for a Wide Range of Foods

One of the key advantages of the Tefal Dual Easy Fry & Grill is its versatility. The appliance can be used to cook a wide variety of foods, from chips and roasted vegetables to grilled meats and fish. It is also capable of baking small cakes and reheating leftovers, making it a multi-purpose tool that can replace several other kitchen appliances. This versatility ensures that you'll get plenty of use out of it, no matter what type of meals you enjoy preparing.

13.Reduced Cooking Time

The Tefal Dual Easy Fry & Grill significantly reduces cooking times compared to traditional methods. Its rapid heating and cooking technology mean that you can prepare meals faster, making it ideal for busy households or those who need to get dinner on the table quickly. Whether you're cooking for yourself or your family, the reduced cooking time allows you to enjoy delicious meals without spending hours in the kitchen.

14.Health-Conscious Grilling

In addition to air frying, the grilling function of the Tefal Dual Easy Fry & Grill allows you to prepare meats and vegetables with a lower fat content. The grill plate is designed to allow excess fat to drain away from the food as it cooks, resulting in healthier meals without sacrificing flavour. This is particularly beneficial for those who want to reduce their intake of saturated fats while still enjoying grilled foods.

15.Ideal for Beginners and Experienced Cooks Alike

Whether you're a seasoned chef or a beginner in the kitchen, the Tefal Dual Easy Fry & Grill is designed to be user-friendly and accessible to all. The pre-set programmes take the guesswork out of cooking, making it easy for novices to prepare meals with confidence. At the same time, experienced cooks will appreciate the adjustable settings and versatility, allowing them to experiment with new recipes and techniques.

Conclusion

In summary, the Tefal Dual Easy Fry & Grill offers a host of benefits that make it an invaluable addition to any

kitchen. Its combination of air frying and grilling provides a healthier, faster, and more versatile way to prepare meals, all while retaining the delicious flavours and textures that make home cooking so enjoyable. With its ease of use, energy efficiency, and stylish design, this appliance caters to both health-conscious individuals and those who simply want to enjoy their favourite foods with less hassle. Whether you're cooking for yourself or your family, the Tefal Dual Easy Fry & Grill is sure to become a staple in your kitchen, simplifying meal preparation and helping you achieve consistently excellent results.

Before First Use

1.Unpack the Appliance: Carefully remove all packaging materials from the Tefal Dual Easy Fry & Grill, including any protective plastic films, foam, or cardboard inserts. Check inside the drawers for any packaging or accessories. Discard all external and internal packaging responsibly.

2.Remove Stickers: Peel off any stickers on the appliance, such as those on the drawer or exterior surfaces. However, ensure you do not remove the QR code sticker, as this may contain important information for registering the product or accessing the manual.

3.Initial Cleaning: Thoroughly clean the appliance before first use. Remove the drawers and any included removable grids. Wash both the drawers and grids with hot water, a small amount of washing-up liquid, and a non-abrasive sponge. Be sure to remove any dust or manufacturing residues. The drawers and grids are dishwasher-safe for your convenience, but you can also wash them by hand if preferred.

4.Wipe the Appliance: Using a soft, damp cloth, wipe down the inside and outside of the appliance. This includes the heating elements, the drawer cavities, and the control panel. Be careful not to use abrasive cleaners or scouring pads, as they may damage the non-stick surfaces or exterior finish.

By following these detailed preparation steps, you will ensure that your Tefal Dual Easy Fry & Grill is clean, safe, and ready for use, providing optimal cooking results from your first use onward.

Preparation for Use

1.Position the Appliance: Place the Tefal Dual Easy Fry & Grill on a flat, stable, and heat-resistant surface. Ensure the appliance is located away from water sources or splashes to avoid potential damage.

2.Clear Surrounding Space: Do not place the appliance in a corner or underneath wall cupboards to prevent overheating. Ensure at least 15 cm of space around the

appliance on all sides to allow proper air circulation. Avoid placing objects on top of the appliance, as this can block airflow and negatively affect cooking performance.

3.Avoid Liquids in the Drawer: Never fill the drawer with oil or any other liquids. This appliance operates through hot air circulation, not deep frying. Adding oil could lead to damage or fire hazards.

4.Clean Components: Before the first use, thoroughly wash the drawers and grids with warm, soapy water and a non-abrasive sponge. The drawers and grids are dishwasher safe for easy cleaning. Ensure all parts are completely dry before use.

5.Power On the Appliance: Press the power button to switch on the appliance. The default mode for Drawer 1 is displayed as "Fries," while Drawer 2 will show as "OFF" unless activated.

6.Select the Desired Drawer: To select a drawer, press the "1" or "2" button depending on which you wish to use. To cancel a selection, press the same button again. The display will show "OFF" when a drawer is deactivated.

7.Ensure Grids Are Inserted: Always place the appropriate grids inside the drawers before cooking to ensure optimal airflow and cooking results.

8.Check Food Quantities: Never exceed the maximum food quantities as indicated in the 'Cooking Guide' section. Overloading the drawers may compromise cooking quality and could prevent proper air circulation.

By following these steps, you ensure safe and efficient operation of your Tefal Dual Easy Fry & Grill.

How to Use It

The UK Tefal Dual Easy Fry & Grill has eight cooking functions such as fries, chicken, vegetables, fish, dessert, dehydrate, manual mode, and grill program. Here's how to use it.

Using Both Drawers in Synchronisation Mode (Dual Cooking)

1.Switching On:

To start, press the Start/Stop button on the control panel to switch on the appliance. By default, the display will show Fries Mode for drawer 1 (the left drawer), while drawer 2 (the right drawer) will show OFF on the screen. This indicates that drawer 1 is active and ready to be set, while drawer 2 needs activation.

2.Setting Drawer 1:

Begin by selecting the desired cooking mode for drawer 1. You can choose from a variety of cooking functions such as fries, grill, roast, or bake. If needed, adjust the cooking time and temperature by pressing the + or - buttons. The settings will be saved once confirmed.

3.Loading Drawer 1:

Once drawer 1 is programmed, place the food item you wish to cook into drawer 1. Ensure the food is spread evenly to allow for proper air circulation. Slide drawer 1 back into the appliance, ensuring it's fully closed and securely in place.

4.Activating Drawer 2:

To use both drawers, press the 2 button on the control panel. This activates drawer 2 and turns the display on for it, allowing you to set the second cooking mode.

5.Setting Drawer 2:

After activating drawer 2, select the cooking mode you wish to use for the food in this drawer. Again, adjust the cooking time and temperature by pressing the + or - buttons as necessary, based on the type of food you are preparing.

6.Loading Drawer 2:

Once drawer 2 is set, place your second food item into the right drawer. As with drawer 1, make sure the food is arranged evenly. Slide drawer 2 back into the appliance securely.

7.Sync Mode:

Press the SYNC button to synchronise the cooking times of both drawers. If the foods you're cooking require different cooking times, the appliance automatically adjusts the start time of the shorter-cooking item. The screen will display HOLD for the shorter cooking mode, indicating that the cooking will be delayed so both drawers finish at the same time. This ensures that both foods are ready to serve simultaneously.

8.Starting Cooking:

After setting both drawers and activating sync mode, press the Start/Stop button to begin the cooking process. The appliance will start cooking according to the programmed settings for each drawer.

9.Completion:

When the cooking is complete, the appliance will beep to signal that both food items are ready at the same time. The sync function ensures that even with different cooking durations, both drawers finish together.

10.Removing Food:

Carefully remove each drawer by sliding them out of the appliance. Use a pair of heat-resistant tongs to remove

the food from the drawers, taking care not to touch the hot surfaces. After use, allow the appliance to cool before cleaning.

By following these detailed steps, you can ensure that the Tefal Dual Easy Fry & Grill delivers perfectly synchronised cooking results for both drawers, making it easy to prepare different types of food simultaneously.

Using Only One Drawer of the Appliance

1.Power On the Appliance:

Press the Start/Stop button to switch on the appliance. The default setting for drawer 1 will display the Fries mode, while drawer 2 will show OFF.

2.Select the Active Drawer:

To activate a drawer, press the 1 or 2 button corresponding to the drawer you wish to use. The other drawer will remain OFF. If you need to cancel the selection, press the 1 or 2 button again.

3.Select Cooking Mode:

Once the drawer is selected, you have two options:

a. Preset Cooking Mode:

- Press the desired cooking mode icon on the touchscreen panel (e.g., fries, chicken, fish).
- Confirm the cooking mode by pressing the Start/Stop button, which will begin the cooking process. The remaining cooking time will be displayed on the screen.

b. Manual Settings:

- Press the MANUAL mode on the touchscreen.
- Adjust the temperature using the + and - buttons (temperature range: 40-200°C).
- Set the cooking time by pressing the + and - buttons (timer range: 0 to 60 minutes).
- Press the Start/Stop button to begin cooking with your selected temperature and time settings. The remaining cooking time will be shown on the screen.

4.Monitor and Shake the Food:

While cooking, excess oil will collect at the bottom of the drawer. Some foods, such as fries, require shaking halfway through cooking to ensure even browning and crispness. When using the Fries mode, an indicator will flash halfway through cooking, prompting you to shake the food.

Pull the drawer out by the handle, shake the contents gently, and slide the drawer back in to resume cooking automatically.

5.End of Cooking Process:

When the cooking time has finished, the appliance will emit a timer sound.

Pull the drawer out and place it on a heat-resistant surface.

Check the food to see if it is cooked to your preference. If more cooking is required, simply slide the drawer back in and adjust the timer for a few additional minutes.

6.Serve the Food:

Once the food is fully cooked, remove the drawer from the appliance. Use tongs to carefully lift the food from the drawer to avoid scratching the non-stick surface.

7.Prepare for the Next Batch:

The Tefal Dual Easy Fry & Grill is ready to cook another batch immediately. If you are preparing multiple dishes, repeat the process as needed.

This detailed step-by-step guide ensures optimal cooking results while maintaining the appliance's performance.

Using Both Drawers on Sync Mode with the Grill Plate

1.Place the Grill Plate: Always place the grill plate in drawer 1 of the appliance.

2.Turn On the Appliance: Press the Start/Stop button. Drawer 1 will default to Fries mode, while drawer 2 will show OFF on the display.

3.Select Grill Mode: Press the GRILL option on the screen to activate Grill mode for drawer Adjust the cooking time if necessary. The temperature is automatically set to 200°C. Do not place food in drawer 1 yet; the grill will begin a preheating phase.

4.Activate Drawer 2: Press '2' on the screen to select

drawer 2. Choose the desired cooking mode (e.g., Fries) and adjust time and temperature as needed.

5.Add Food to Drawer 2: Place your food into drawer 2 and slide it back into the appliance.

6.Press SYNC: Activate Sync mode by pressing SYNC. This ensures both drawers finish cooking simultaneously.

7.Start Cooking: Press the Start/Stop button to initiate the cooking process. Drawer 1 will begin preheating for grilling, and the grill light will turn on, with "Pre Heat" displayed on the screen.

8.End of Preheating: When the preheating is complete, you will hear a timer sound, and the screen will display 'Add'.

9.Add Food to Grill Plate: Take out drawer 1 and place it on a heat-resistant surface. Place the food onto the grill plate and return the drawer to the appliance.

10.Cooking Begins Automatically: Once the food is in place, the cooking process starts automatically, and the remaining cooking time is displayed on the screen.

11.End of Cooking: When the cooking time ends, the timer will sound, indicating that both drawers have finished cooking.

12.Remove the Drawers: Take both drawers out of the appliance and place them on a heat-resistant surface.

13.Serve the Food: Use a pair of tongs to carefully lift the food from both drawers.

This process allows you to synchronise cooking in both drawers while using the grill plate for optimal results.

Tips for Using Accessories

1.Grill Plate Usage

The grill plate is perfect for searing meats, fish, and vegetables, providing those classic grill marks and enhancing the flavours of your food. Always ensure the grill plate is preheated before placing your ingredients. This not only speeds up the cooking process but also helps in achieving the desired char and texture. Additionally, avoid overcrowding the grill plate to allow proper air circulation, ensuring even cooking.

2.Crisper Basket Efficiency

The crisper basket is ideal for achieving perfectly crisp results with foods like chips, chicken wings, and other fried favourites. Ensure that food is spread evenly within the basket and avoid overloading it. Overfilling the basket can prevent air from circulating properly, which may result in uneven cooking. For best results, shake the crisper basket halfway through cooking to redistribute the food, ensuring an even, golden-brown finish.

3.Removable Grids for Easy Cleaning

The removable grids are designed to elevate food from the base, allowing fat and excess oil to drain away during cooking. For healthier meals, always use these grids when grilling or air frying meats. After each use, ensure that the grids are cleaned thoroughly with warm, soapy water or placed in the dishwasher, as they are dishwasher-safe. Regular cleaning will prevent the buildup of grease, ensuring your food remains fresh and the appliance operates at peak efficiency.

4.Baking with the Adjustable Rack

For those who enjoy baking, the adjustable rack allows for more versatile cooking options. You can use this accessory to cook multiple items at once or adjust the height to suit different recipes, from cakes to pizzas. When using the rack, be sure to check on your food periodically to prevent overcooking, particularly with baked goods that may require less time than traditional frying.

5.Using the Drip Tray

The drip tray is designed to collect excess oils and juices that drip during cooking, especially when grilling. Always place it in the correct position beneath the food to ensure a cleaner cooking process. After use, empty and clean the drip tray to prevent grease buildup, which could affect the appliance's performance over time.

By following these tips, you'll maximise the versatility and efficiency of your Tefal Dual Easy Fry & Grill, ensuring delicious, healthy meals every time.

Cleaning and Caring for Tefal Dual Easy Fry & Grill

Routine cleaning and maintenance of your equipment is the secret to its longevity. Below are steps on how to clean and maintain your equipment on a daily basis.

1.Unplug and Cool Down

Always unplug the appliance and allow it to cool down completely before starting the cleaning process. This ensures safety and prevents any risk of burns or damage to the device.

2.Remove and Clean the Drawers

Carefully remove the drawers and grids from the appliance. Both are dishwasher safe, but they can also be cleaned manually using warm water, some mild washing-up liquid, and a non-abrasive sponge to prevent scratches. Rinse thoroughly and dry completely before placing them back.

3.Wipe the Heating Elements

Use a soft, damp cloth to carefully wipe the inside of the appliance, particularly around the heating elements. Be gentle to avoid damaging these components, and ensure they are completely dry before use.

4.Clean the Exterior

The exterior of the Tefal Dual Easy Fry & Grill should be wiped down with a damp cloth or sponge. Avoid using abrasive materials that can damage the finish of the appliance. Dry it with a soft cloth to prevent streaks.

5.Avoid Using Harsh Chemicals

Refrain from using harsh cleaning agents or chemicals, as these may damage the non-stick coating or internal components of the appliance. Stick to mild detergents and non-abrasive sponges for best results.

6.Maintain Ventilation

Keep the air vents clear of dust and debris to maintain optimal airflow during operation. You can use a soft brush or cloth to clean the vent area.

7.Regular Maintenance

For optimal performance, clean the appliance after each use. Regular maintenance will prolong its lifespan and ensure that it continues to function efficiently.

8.Storage

Ensure the appliance is completely dry before storing it away. Store it in a cool, dry place, and avoid placing any heavy items on top to prevent damage to the grill or drawer. Proper care of your Tefal Dual Easy Fry & Grill ensures better performance and longevity.

Frequently Asked Questions & Notes

1.Can I use oil in the Tefal Dual Easy Fry & Grill?

No, the Tefal Dual Easy Fry & Grill operates using hot air circulation for cooking, so it is not necessary to fill the drawer with oil or any other liquid. However, you may lightly coat food with oil for a crispier texture if desired. It's important to avoid using too much oil, as this can cause excess smoke.

2.Are the drawers and grids dishwasher safe?

Yes, the removable drawers and grids of the Tefal Dual Easy Fry & Grill are dishwasher safe. You can safely clean them using a mild detergent in the dishwasher, making cleanup after cooking more convenient. However, if you prefer, you can hand-wash them with warm water and a non-abrasive sponge to maintain the integrity of the non-stick coating.

3.Can I cook two different foods at once?

Absolutely! The Tefal Dual Easy Fry & Grill is designed with dual cooking zones, allowing you to prepare two different foods simultaneously. Each drawer has independent cooking controls, so you can select different times and temperatures for each side. This makes it easy to cook various dishes like chips and chicken without cross-contamination.

4.Do I need to preheat the appliance?

Preheating is not always required but may help achieve better cooking results, particularly for baking or grilling. If a recipe calls for preheating, simply select the desired temperature and let the appliance heat up for a few minutes before placing your food in the drawers. The screen will indicate when preheating is complete.

5.How do I adjust the cooking time and temperature?

The Tefal Dual Easy Fry & Grill is equipped with easy-to-use controls. Use the "+" and "–" buttons on the display to adjust the time and temperature. Each drawer operates independently, so you can modify the settings for each cooking zone based on what you're preparing. Refer to the cooking guide in the user manual for recommended settings for specific foods.

6.How can I prevent food from sticking to the grids?

To prevent food from sticking, you can lightly coat the grids with a cooking spray or oil before placing the food in the drawer. Ensure you don't use excessive oil, as the appliance is designed for minimal-oil cooking. Additionally, always clean the grids thoroughly after each use to remove any residual food or oil that may lead to sticking in future cooking sessions.

7.What is the maximum amount of food I can place in each drawer?

Each drawer has a maximum food capacity, which is outlined in the "Cooking Guide" section of the manual. Overloading the drawers may result in uneven cooking, so it's essential not to exceed the recommended quantities. Allow enough space for the hot air to circulate properly around the food to ensure it cooks evenly.

8.Can I open the drawer while cooking to check on the food?

Yes, you can open the drawer at any point during cooking to check on your food or shake it for more even cooking. The appliance will pause automatically when the drawer is removed and will resume once the drawer is reinserted. For certain foods, such as chips or roasted vegetables, shaking halfway through cooking helps achieve a more uniform crispness.

9.How do I use the grill function?

To use the grill function, select the "Grill" mode from the control panel, adjust the temperature, and preheat the appliance if necessary. Place your food on the suitable grill plate inside the drawer and start cooking. The grill function is perfect for achieving a nice sear on steaks, fish, or vegetables, ensuring delicious grilled flavour without the need for an outdoor grill.

10.How do I clean the appliance?

For cleaning, remove the drawers and grids and wash them in warm, soapy water or place them in the dishwasher. Wipe the inside and outside of the appliance with a damp cloth, making sure to remove any food residues. Avoid using abrasive cleaning products or scouring pads, as these may damage the non-stick surfaces. Ensure the appliance is completely dry before storage.

11.What should I do if the appliance produces too much smoke?

If your Tefal Dual Easy Fry & Grill is emitting excess smoke, it could be due to leftover food or oil residue inside the drawer or on the heating element. Make sure to clean the appliance thoroughly after each use. If cooking particularly fatty foods, consider placing a small amount of water in the drawer to reduce smoke. Also, ensure that you are not exceeding the recommended amount of oil.

12.How do I ensure my food cooks evenly?

To ensure even cooking, spread food out in a single layer and avoid overcrowding the drawers. Shaking the food halfway through cooking (for items like chips or nuggets) also helps achieve uniform results. Always follow the temperature and time guidelines provided in the "Cooking Guide" for best results.

13.Can I cook frozen foods in the appliance?

Yes, frozen foods such as chips, fish fingers, and chicken nuggets can be cooked in the Tefal Dual Easy Fry & Grill. Simply adjust the cooking time and temperature as needed. There's no need to defrost most frozen foods before cooking, as the hot air circulation will ensure they cook thoroughly and evenly.

14.What safety precautions should I follow?

Always ensure the appliance is placed on a flat, heat-resistant surface away from water sources. Avoid placing any objects on top of the appliance, as this can interfere with airflow and cause overheating. When removing drawers during cooking, be cautious of the hot surfaces and use oven gloves if necessary. Keep the appliance out of reach of children during use.

15.How do I store the appliance?

Once the appliance is clean and dry, store it in a cool, dry place. If space permits, keep the drawers slightly ajar to prevent odours and moisture build-up. Avoid wrapping the power cord tightly around the appliance to prevent damage to the cord.

4-Week Meal Plan

Week 1

Day 1:

Breakfast: Breakfast Potato-Kale Patties
Lunch: Roasted Garlic Asparagus
Snack: Fried Green Tomatoes with Horseradish Drizzle
Dinner: Southern Fried Chicken Drumsticks
Dessert: Baked Apples

Day 2:

Breakfast: Fluffy Honey Cornbread
Lunch: Baked Hasselback Potatoes
Snack: Fried Dill Pickles
Dinner: Shrimp Kebabs
Dessert: Sweet Caramelised Mixed Nut

Day 3:

Breakfast: Crispy Potato Flautas
Lunch: Grilled Corn On The Cob
Snack: Herbed Pita Chips
Dinner: Hamburger Steak with Mushroom Gravy
Dessert: Small Batch Brownies

Day 4:

Breakfast: Fried Donut Holes
Lunch: Garlic-Roasted Red Potatoes
Snack: Garlic Parmesan Chicken Wings
Dinner: Chicken Cordon Bleu Casserole
Dessert: Shortbread Cake

Day 5:

Breakfast: Banana Chia Bread
Lunch: Cauliflower Fried Rice
Snack: Roasted Mixed Nuts
Dinner: Crab Cakes with Lemon Aioli
Dessert: Apple Pie Taquitos

Day 6:

Breakfast: Tempeh and Veggie Scramble
Lunch: Roasted Vegetable Medley
Snack: Tomato and Basil Bruschetta
Dinner: Southern-Style Cola Meat Loaf
Dessert: Grilled Peanut Butter S'Mores Sandwiches

Day 7:

Breakfast: Breakfast Pancake
Lunch: Fried Breaded Okra
Snack: Sausage Rolls
Dinner: Pork Chops with Caramelised Onions and Peppers
Dessert: Blueberry Cake

Week 2

Day 1:

Breakfast: Apple and Berry Breakfast Crumble
Lunch: Crispy Salty Tofu
Snack: Mozzarella Sticks
Dinner: The Best Chicken Fajitas
Dessert: Banana Spring Rolls

Day 2:

Breakfast: Homemade Fried Biscuits
Lunch: Air Fried Spiced Acorn Squash
Snack: Healthy Carrot Chips
Dinner: Crispy Coconut Shrimp with Spicy Dipping Sauce
Dessert: Savoury Pear Pecan Crostata

Day 3:

Breakfast: Marinated Tempeh Bacon
Lunch: Brussels Sprouts with Bacon
Snack: Crispy Breaded Artichoke Hearts
Dinner: Beef and Broccoli Stir-Fry
Dessert: Carrot Cake in a Mug

Day 4:

Breakfast: Fluffy Honey Cornbread
Lunch: Bacon-Wrapped Asparagus
Snack: Garlic Sweet Potato Fries
Dinner: Flavourful Cobb Salad
Dessert: White Chocolate Blondies

Day 5:

Breakfast: Fried Donut Holes
Lunch: Crispy Breaded Fried Aubergine
Snack: Buffalo Breaded Cauliflower Bites
Dinner: Lemony Butter Cod
Dessert: Pistachio Baked Pears

Day 6:

Breakfast: Banana Chia Bread
Lunch: Roasted Garlic Asparagus
Snack: Fried Green Tomatoes with Horseradish Drizzle
Dinner: Beef Empanadas
Dessert: Baked Apples

Day 7:

Breakfast: Breakfast Potato-Kale Patties
Lunch: Baked Hasselback Potatoes
Snack: Fried Dill Pickles
Dinner: Barbecue Pork Chops
Dessert: Sweet Caramelised Mixed Nut

Week 3

Day 1:

Breakfast: Crispy Potato Flautas
Lunch: Grilled Corn On The Cob
Snack: Herbed Pita Chips
Dinner: Crispy Duck with Cherry Sauce
Dessert: Apple Pie Taquitos

Day 2:

Breakfast: Tempeh and Veggie Scramble
Lunch: Garlic-Roasted Red Potatoes
Snack: Garlic Parmesan Chicken Wings
Dinner: Classic Fish and "Chips"
Dessert: Shortbread Cake

Day 3:

Breakfast: Breakfast Pancake
Lunch: Cauliflower Fried Rice
Snack: Roasted Mixed Nuts
Dinner: Parmesan-Crusted Steak
Dessert: Grilled Peanut Butter S'Mores Sandwiches

Day 4:

Breakfast: Homemade Fried Biscuits
Lunch: Roasted Vegetable Medley
Snack: Tomato and Basil Bruschetta
Dinner: Jalapeño Popper Chicken Breasts
Dessert: Small Batch Brownies

Day 5:

Breakfast: Marinated Tempeh Bacon
Lunch: Fried Breaded Okra
Snack: Sausage Rolls
Dinner: Black Cod with Grapes, Fennel, Pecans, and Kale
Dessert: Blueberry Cake

Day 6:

Breakfast: Apple and Berry Breakfast Crumble
Lunch: Crispy Salty Tofu
Snack: Mozzarella Sticks
Dinner: Greek Meatballs with Tzatziki Sauce
Dessert: Banana Spring Rolls

Day 7:

Breakfast: Fluffy Honey Cornbread
Lunch: Air Fried Spiced Acorn Squash
Snack: Healthy Carrot Chips
Dinner: Barbecue Pulled Pork Sandwiches
Dessert: Savoury Pear Pecan Crostata

Week 4

Day 1:

Breakfast: Fried Donut Holes
Lunch: Brussels Sprouts with Bacon
Snack: Crispy Breaded Artichoke Hearts
Dinner: Apricot Glazed Chicken Thighs
Dessert: White Chocolate Blondies

Day 2:

Breakfast: Banana Chia Bread
Lunch: Bacon-Wrapped Asparagus
Snack: Garlic Sweet Potato Fries
Dinner: Shrimp Spring Rolls
Dessert: Pistachio Baked Pears

Day 3:

Breakfast: Breakfast Potato-Kale Patties
Lunch: Crispy Breaded Fried Aubergine
Snack: Buffalo Breaded Cauliflower Bites
Dinner: Thai Beef Satay with Peanut Sauce
Dessert: Baked Apples

Day 4:

Breakfast: Crispy Potato Flautas
Lunch: Roasted Garlic Asparagus
Snack: Fried Green Tomatoes with Horseradish Drizzle
Dinner: Turkey Breast with Cherry Glaze
Dessert: Sweet Caramelised Mixed Nut

Day 5:

Breakfast: Tempeh and Veggie Scramble
Lunch: Baked Hasselback Potatoes
Snack: Fried Dill Pickles
Dinner: Crispy Breaded Calamari
Dessert: Apple Pie Taquitos

Day 6:

Breakfast: Breakfast Pancake
Lunch: Grilled Corn On The Cob
Snack: Herbed Pita Chips
Dinner: London Broil with Herb Butter
Dessert: Shortbread Cake

Day 7:

Breakfast: Homemade Fried Biscuits
Lunch: Garlic-Roasted Red Potatoes
Snack: Garlic Parmesan Chicken Wings
Dinner: Porcupine Meatballs
Dessert: Small Batch Brownies

Chapter 1 Breakfast

Fluffy Honey Cornbread

Prep Time: 5 minutes **Cook: 20-24 minutes** **Serves: 4**

120g all-purpose flour
130g yellow cornmeal
100g sugar
1 teaspoon salt
2 teaspoons baking powder
1 large egg
240ml milk
160ml vegetable oil
85g honey

1. Spray a baking pan (square or round) that fits your appliance with olive oil or cooking spray. 2. In a large mixing bowl, add the flour, cornmeal, baking powder, egg, sugar, salt, milk, oil, and honey and mix lightly. 3. Pour the cornbread batter into the prepared pan. 4. Press the Start/Stop button to switch on the appliance. To activate the drawer 1, press '1' button. Press MANUAL mode. Adjust the temperature to 180°C and time for 20 minutes. 5. Place the baking pan in the drawer 1 and slide the drawer back into appliance. Press the Start/Stop button to begin cooking. 6. Insert a toothpick into the centre of the cornbread to make sure the middle is cooked; if not, bake for another 3 to 4 minutes. 7. Using silicone oven mitts, remove the pan from the appliance and let cool slightly. Serve warm.

Fried Donut Holes

Prep Time: 15 minutes **Cook: 16 minutes** **Serves: 4-6**

1 tablespoon ground flaxseed
1½ tablespoons water
60ml nondairy milk, unsweetened
2 tablespoons neutral-flavoured oil (sunflower, safflower, or refined coconut)
1½ teaspoons vanilla
180g whole-wheat pastry flour or all-purpose gluten-free flour
145g coconut sugar, divided
2½ teaspoons cinnamon, divided
½ teaspoon nutmeg
¼ teaspoon sea salt
¾ teaspoon baking powder
Cooking oil spray (refined coconut, sunflower, or safflower)

1. In a medium bowl, stir the flaxseed with the water and set aside for 5 minutes, or until gooey and thick. 2. Add the milk, oil, and vanilla. Stir well and set this wet mixture aside. 3. In a small bowl, add the flour, ½ teaspoon cinnamon, the nutmeg, salt, 95g coconut sugar, and the baking powder. Stir very well. Add this mixture to the wet mixture and stir together—it will be stiff, so you'll need to knead it lightly, just until all of the ingredients are thoroughly combined. 4. Spray the drawer with oil. Pull off bits of the dough and roll into 1 inch balls. Place 12 balls in the drawer, leaving room in between as they'll increase in size a smidge, and spray the tops with oil. 5. Press the Start/Stop button to switch on the appliance. To activate the drawer 1, press '1' button. Press MANUAL mode. Adjust the temperature to 175°C and time for 2 minutes. 6. Slide the drawer back into appliance and press the Start/Stop button to begin cooking. 7. Remove the drawer, spray the donut holes with oil again, flip them over, and spray them with oil again. Fry them for 2 more minutes, or until golden-brown. 8. During these last 2 minutes of frying, place the remaining 4 tablespoons coconut sugar and 2 teaspoons cinnamon in a bowl and stir to combine. 9. When the donut holes are done frying, remove them one at a time and coat them as follows: Spray with oil again and toss with the cinnamon-sugar mixture. Spray one last time and coat with the cinnamon-sugar one last time. Enjoy fresh and warm if possible, as they're best that way.

Banana Chia Bread

Prep Time: 10 minutes **Cook: 25 minutes** **Serves: 6**

2 large bananas, very ripe, peeled, mashed banana
2 tablespoons neutral-flavoured oil (sunflower or safflower)
2 tablespoons maple syrup
½ teaspoon vanilla
½ tablespoon chia seeds
½ tablespoon ground flaxseed
120g whole-wheat pastry flour
50g coconut sugar
½ teaspoon cinnamon
¼ teaspoon salt
¼ teaspoon nutmeg
¼ teaspoon baking powder
¼ teaspoon baking soda
Cooking oil spray (sunflower, safflower, or refined coconut)

1. In a medium bowl, mash the peeled bananas with a fork until very mushy. Add the oil, vanilla, chia, maple syrup, and flaxseeds and stir well. 2. Add the flour, sugar, nutmeg, baking powder, cinnamon, salt, and baking soda, and stir just until thoroughly combined. 3. Press the Start/Stop button to switch on the appliance. To activate the drawer 1, press '1' button. Press MANUAL mode. Adjust the temperature to 175°C and time for 2 minutes. 4. Place a baking pan that fits your appliance food in the drawer 1 and slide the drawer back into appliance. Press the Start/Stop button to begin cooking. 5. After preheat the baking pan for 2 minutes, remove the drawer, spray the baking pan with oil, and pour the batter into the baking pan. Smooth out the top with a rubber spatula and bake for 25 minutes, or until a knife inserted in the centre comes out clean. 6. Remove the pan and let cool for a minute or two, then cut into wedges or slices and serve.

Breakfast Potato-Kale Patties

Prep Time: 10 minutes **Cook: 40 minutes** **Serves: 5**

4 small potatoes (russet or Yukon Gold)
40g (lightly packed) kale, stems removed and finely chopped
90g chickpea flour
10g nutritional yeast
180ml oat milk, plain and unsweetened (or your nondairy milk of choice)
2 tablespoons fresh lemon juice
2 teaspoons dried rosemary
2 teaspoons onion granules
1 teaspoon sea salt
½ teaspoon freshly ground black pepper
½ teaspoon turmeric powder
Cooking oil spray (sunflower, safflower, or refined coconut)

1. Scrub the potatoes, leaving the skins on for maximum nutrition. 2. Press the Start/Stop button to switch on the appliance. To activate the drawer 1, press '1' button. Press MANUAL mode. Adjust the temperature to 200°C and time for 30 minutes. 3. Place the potatoes in the drawer 1 and slide the drawer back into appliance. Press the Start/Stop button to begin cooking. Cook for 30 minutes, or until tender. 4. When cool enough to handle, chop the cooked potatoes into small pieces, place in a large bowl, and mash them with a potato masher or fork. Add the yeast, kale, milk, lemon, rosemary, chickpea flour, onion granules, pepper, salt, and turmeric and stir well, until thoroughly combined. 5. Spray the drawer with oil and set aside. 4. Remove ¼ cup of batter and roll it into a ball with your hands. Smash it into a ½-inch thick patty, about 3 inches in diameter, and place in the drawer. Repeat with the remaining batter, taking care not to overlap the patties in the drawer, and spray the tops with oil. You may need to do this in batches. 6. Slide the drawer back into appliance and press the Start/Stop button to begin cooking. Cook at 200°C for 5 minutes. 7. Remove the drawer, spray the tops again, and flip each patty over. Spray the tops with oil and cook for another 5 minutes, or until gorgeously golden-brown and cooked through. 8. Remove, and serve plain or with cheesy sauce. Leftover batter will stay fresh in an airtight container, refrigerated, for about 5 days.

Crispy Potato Flautas

Prep Time: 20 minutes Cook: 8 minutes Serves: 2

1 medium potato, peeled and chopped into small cubes (225g chopped potato)
2 tablespoons nondairy milk, plain and unsweetened
2 large garlic cloves, minced or pressed
¼ teaspoon sea salt
⅛ teaspoon freshly ground black pepper
2 tablespoons minced scallions
4 sprouted corn tortillas
Cooking oil spray (sunflower, safflower, or refined coconut)
Green Chilli Sauce or fresh salsa
Guacamole or fresh avocado slices (optional)
Cilantro, minced (optional)

1. In a pot on the stovetop fitted with a steamer basket, cook the potato cubes for 15 minutes, or until tender. 2. Transfer the cooked potato cubes to a bowl and mash with a potato masher or fork. Add the milk, salt, garlic, and pepper and stir well. Add the scallions and stir them into the mixture. Set the bowl aside. 3. Run the tortillas under water for a second and then place them in an oil-sprayed drawer (stacking them is fine). 4. Press the Start/Stop button to switch on the appliance. To activate the drawer 1, press '1' button. Press MANUAL mode. Adjust the temperature to 200°C and time for 1 minute. 5. Slide the drawer back into appliance and press the Start/Stop button to begin cooking. 6. Transfer the tortillas to a flat surface, laying them out individually. Place an equal amount of the potato filling in the centre of each tortilla. Roll the tortilla sides up over the filling and place seam-side down in the drawer (this helps prevent the tortillas from flying open). Spray the tops with oil. Slide the drawer back into appliance and press the Start/Stop button to begin cooking. Cook at 200°C for 7 minutes, or until the tortillas are golden-browned and lightly crisp. 7. Serve with sauce or salsa, and any of the additional options as desired. Enjoy immediately.

Tempeh and Veggie Scramble

Prep Time: 10 minutes Cook: 23 minutes Serves: 4

230g tempeh
2 cloves garlic, minced
1 teaspoon ground turmeric
1 teaspoon ground cumin
½ teaspoon chilli powder
½ teaspoon black salt
60ml to 120ml low-sodium vegetable broth
1 to 2 spritzes extra-virgin olive oil
230g coarsely chopped cremini mushrooms (or your favourite mushroom)
1 small red onion, quartered
55g coarsely chopped bell pepper (any color)
75g sliced cherry or grape tomatoes

1. Steam the tempeh for 10 minutes. (This step is optional, but I'm a huge fan of steaming tempeh in advance to help it absorb marinade, tame its bitterness, and soften its texture a bit.) Cut the tempeh into 12 equal cubes. 2. In a shallow bowl, combine the garlic, turmeric, cumin, black salt, chilli powder, and broth. Add the steamed tempeh and marinate for a minimum of 30 minutes or up to overnight. 3. Spray the drawer with the oil. Drain the tempeh and add it to the drawer. Add the mushrooms, onion, and bell pepper. 4. Press the Start/Stop button to switch on the appliance. To activate the drawer 1, press '1' button. Press MANUAL mode. Adjust the temperature to 165°C and time for 10 minutes. 5. Slide the drawer back into appliance and press the Start/Stop button to begin cooking. 6. Add the tomatoes, increase the heat to 200°C and cook 3 more minutes. 7. When done, stir to combine and serve.

Breakfast Pancake

Prep Time: 10 minutes Cook: 12-14 minutes Serves: 2

60g unbleached all-purpose flour
2 tablespoons coconut sugar or granulated sugar
1 tablespoon baking powder
1 to 2 pinches sea salt
120ml soymilk or other nondairy milk
1 tablespoon applesauce
¼ teaspoon vanilla extract
1 to 2 spritzes extra-virgin olive oil spray

1. Combine the flour, baking powder, salt, and sugar in a mixing bowl. Slowly whisk in the milk, applesauce, and vanilla extract. 2. Grease a springform pan (or an oven-safe dish of your choice) with the olive oil spray and pour the batter into the pan. 3. Press the Start/Stop button to switch on the appliance. To activate the drawer 1, press '1' button. Press MANUAL mode. Adjust the temperature to 165°C and time for 10 minutes. 4. Place the springform pan in the drawer 1 and slide the drawer back into appliance. Press the Start/Stop button to begin cooking. 5. Insert a toothpick into the centre to check for doneness—it should come out dry. Cook for another 2 to 4 minutes as needed. 6. When done, serve and enjoy.

Homemade Fried Biscuits

Prep Time: 10 minutes Cook: 7 minutes Serves: 4

120ml almond milk
1½ teaspoons fresh lemon juice
120g unbleached all-purpose flour
1½ teaspoons baking powder
¼ teaspoon baking soda
½ teaspoon sea salt
2 tablespoons plus 2 teaspoons cold nondairy butter

1. In a small bowl, add the milk and lemon juice and refrigerate for 10 minutes. 2. In large bowl, combine the flour, baking soda, baking powder, and salt, and mix well. Use a knife to cut the butter into small pieces in the bowl and then break them up into the flour mixture. To avoid melting the butter, quickly mix the butter and flour together. Continue mixing until the mixture resembles bread crumbs. Add the chilled milk mixture and combine with a wooden spoon until a dough has formed. 3. Transfer the dough to a floured work surface. Dust the top of the dough with additional flour and fold and press it 5 or 6 times, until you achieve a circle of dough about 1 inch thick. Use a biscuit cutter or circular mould to cut out 4 biscuits from the dough. Do this by pressing straight down through the dough. Place the biscuits close in the drawer, so that they are barely touching. Continue to reform the remaining dough to make additional biscuits. Do this quickly as overhandling the dough could impact how the biscuits rise. 4. Press the Start/Stop button to switch on the appliance. To activate the drawer 1, press '1' button. Press MANUAL mode. Adjust the temperature to 200°C and time for 7 minutes. Slide the drawer back into appliance and press the Start/Stop button to begin cooking. Cook until golden brown. 5. When done, serve and enjoy.

Marinated Tempeh Bacon

Prep Time: 10 minutes Cook: 23 minutes Serves: 4

225g tempeh
2 tablespoons maple syrup
1 teaspoon avocado oil or extra-virgin olive oil
½ teaspoon vegan Worcestershire sauce, tamari, or soy sauce
⅛ teaspoon liquid smoke
½ teaspoon cayenne pepper

1. Steam the tempeh for 10 minutes. Transfer the tempeh to a shallow bowl. 2. In a small bowl, combine the maple syrup, liquid smoke, oil, Worcestershire sauce, and cayenne, whisking until well blended. Pour the marinade over the tempeh and marinate for at least 1 hour or overnight. 3. Place the tempeh slices in the drawer. 4. Press the Start/Stop button to switch on the appliance. To activate the drawer 1, press '1' button. Press MANUAL mode. Adjust the temperature to 165°C and time for 10 minutes. 5. Slide the drawer back into appliance and press the Start/Stop button to begin cooking. 6. Shake after 5 minutes. Increase the heat to 200°C and cook for 3 minutes longer. 7. When done, serve and enjoy.

Apple and Berry Breakfast Crumble

Prep Time: 15 minutes Cook: 20 minutes Serves: 4

1 large Granny Smith apple, peeled and chopped
75g chopped strawberries
40g raspberries
1 tablespoon freshly squeezed lemon juice
2 tablespoons granulated sugar
40g rolled oats
65g brown sugar
55g butter, at room temperature
30g all-purpose flour
½ teaspoon cinnamon
Pinch sea salt

1. In a round pan that fits your appliance, combine the apple, strawberries, and raspberries. Drizzle with the lemon juice, sprinkle with the sugar, and toss to mix. 2. In a medium bowl, combine the oats, cinnamon, brown sugar, butter, flour, and salt and mix until crumbly, like coarse sand. 3. Sprinkle the oat mixture over the fruit in the pan. 4. Press the Start/Stop button to switch on the appliance. To activate the drawer 1, press '1' button. Press MANUAL mode. Adjust the temperature to 160°C and time for 15 minutes. 5. Place the pan in the drawer 1 and slide the drawer back into appliance. Press the Start/Stop button to begin cooking. 6. Cook for 15 to 20 minutes, checking after 15 minutes, until the topping is golden brown and the fruit is bubbling. 7. Let cool for 20 minutes, then serve.

Chapter 2 Vegetables and Sides

Roasted Garlic Asparagus

Prep Time: 5 minutes **Cook: 10 minutes** **Serves: 4**

455g asparagus
2 tablespoons olive oil
1 tablespoon balsamic vinegar
2 teaspoons minced garlic
Salt
Freshly ground black pepper

1. Cut or snap off the white end of the asparagus. 2. In a large bowl, combine the asparagus, vinegar, garlic, salt, olive oil, and pepper. 3. Using your hands, gently mix all the ingredients together, making sure that the asparagus is thoroughly coated. 4. Lay out the asparagus in the drawer. 5. Press the Start/Stop button to switch on the appliance. To activate the drawer 1, press '1' button. Press MANUAL mode. Adjust the temperature to 200°C and time for 5 minutes. 6. Slide the drawer back into appliance and press the Start/Stop button to begin cooking. 7. Using tongs, flip the asparagus and roast for 5 minutes more. 8. When done, serve and enjoy.

Baked Hasselback Potatoes

Prep Time: 10 minutes **Cook: 35 minutes** **Serves: 4**

4 russet potatoes
2 tablespoons olive oil
1 teaspoon salt
½ teaspoon freshly ground black pepper
25g grated Parmesan cheese

1. Without cutting through the bottom of the potato (so that the slices stay attached), cut each potato into ½-inch-wide horizontal slices. 2. Brush the potatoes thoroughly with the olive oil, being careful to brush in between all the slices. Season with the salt and pepper. 3. Place the potatoes in the drawer. 4. Press the Start/Stop button to switch on the appliance. To activate the drawer 1, press '1' button. Press MANUAL mode. Adjust the temperature to 175°C and time for 20 minutes. Slide the drawer back into appliance and press the Start/Stop button to begin cooking. 5. Remove the drawer, brush more olive oil onto the potatoes, and bake for 15 minutes more. 6. Remove the potatoes when they are fork-tender. Sprinkle the cooked potatoes with the salt, pepper, and Parmesan cheese.

Grilled Corn On The Cob

Prep Time: 5 minutes Cook: 10 minutes Serves: 4

1 tablespoon vegetable oil
4 ears of corn, husks and silk removed
Unsalted butter, for topping
Salt, for topping
Freshly ground black pepper, for topping

1. Rub the vegetable oil onto the corn, coating it thoroughly. 2. Place the grill plate in the drawer 1 of the appliance. Press the Start/Stop button to switch on the appliance. Press the GRILL button to select the Grill mode and adjust the cooking time for 5 minutes. The temperature is automatically set at 200°C. 3. Start the preheating by pressing the Start/Stop button. 4. When the preheating phase has finished, take the drawer 1 out the appliance. Place the corns on the grill plate and put back the drawer into the appliance. The cooking starts automatically. 5. Using tongs, flip or rotate the corn, and grill for 5 minutes more. 6. Serve with a pat of butter and a generous sprinkle of salt and pepper.

Garlic-Roasted Red Potatoes

Prep Time: 5 minutes Cook: 20 minutes Serves: 4

6 red potatoes, cut into 1-inch cubes
3 garlic cloves, minced
Salt
Pepper
1 teaspoon chopped chives
1 tablespoon extra-virgin olive oil

1. In a sealable plastic bag, combine the potatoes, garlic, salt and pepper to taste, chives, and olive oil. Seal the bag and shake to coat the potatoes. 2. Transfer the potatoes to the drawer. 3. Press the Start/Stop button to switch on the appliance. To activate the drawer 1, press '1' button. Press MANUAL mode. Adjust the temperature to 185°C and time for 10 minutes. Slide the drawer back into appliance and press the Start/Stop button to begin cooking. 4. Remove the drawer, shake, and cook for another 10 minutes. 5. When done, let cool before serving.

Cauliflower Fried Rice

Prep Time: 25 minutes **Cook: 20 minutes** **Serves: 5**

285g riced cauliflower (1 head cauliflower if making your own)
2 teaspoons sesame oil, divided
1 medium green bell pepper, chopped
145g peas
115g diced carrots
65g chopped onion
Salt
Pepper
1 tablespoon soy sauce
2 medium eggs, scrambled

1. If you choose to make your own riced cauliflower, grate the head of cauliflower using the medium-size holes of a cheese grater. Or you can cut the head of cauliflower into florets and pulse in a food processer until it has the appearance of rice. 2. Coat the bottom of drawer with 1 teaspoon of sesame oil. 3. In a large bowl, combine the riced cauliflower, peas, carrots, green bell pepper, and onion. Drizzle the remaining 1 teaspoon of sesame oil over the vegetables and stir. Add the salt and pepper to taste. 4. Transfer the mixture to the drawer. 5. Press the Start/Stop button to switch on the appliance. To activate the drawer 1, press '1' button. Press MANUAL mode. Adjust the temperature to 190°C and time for 10 minutes. Slide the drawer back into appliance and press the Start/Stop button to begin cooking. 6. Remove the drawer, drizzle the soy sauce all over, and add the scrambled eggs. Stir to combine. 7. When done, serve warm.

Roasted Vegetable Medley

Prep Time: 5 minutes **Cook: 12 minutes** **Serves: 4**

1 head broccoli, chopped (about 200g)
2 medium carrots, cut into 1-inch pieces
Salt
Pepper
Cooking oil
1 courgette, cut into 1-inch chunks
1 medium red bell pepper, seeded and thinly sliced

1. In a large bowl, combine the broccoli and carrots. Season with the salt and pepper to taste and spray with the cooking oil. 2. Transfer the broccoli and carrots to the drawer. 3. Press the Start/Stop button to switch on the appliance. To activate the drawer 1, press '1' button. Press MANUAL mode. Adjust the temperature to 200°C and time for 6 minutes. Slide the drawer back into appliance and press the Start/Stop button to begin cooking. 4. Place the courgette and red pepper in the bowl. Season with the salt and pepper to taste and spray with the cooking oil. 5. Add the courgette and red pepper to the broccoli and carrots in the drawer. Cook for 6 minutes. 6. When done, let cool before serving.

Fried Breaded Okra

Prep Time: 15 minutes Cook: 10 minutes Serves: 4

150g okra, cut into ¼-inch pieces
3 tablespoons buttermilk
2 tablespoons all-purpose flour
2 tablespoons cornmeal
Salt
Pepper
Cooking oil

1. Make sure the okra pieces are dry, using paper towels if needed. 2. Pour the buttermilk into a small bowl. In another small bowl, combine the flour and cornmeal and season with the salt and pepper to taste. 3. Spray the drawer with cooking oil. 4. Dip the okra in the buttermilk, then the flour and cornmeal. 5. Place the okra in the drawer. It is okay to stack it. Spray the okra with cooking oil. 6. Press the Start/Stop button to switch on the appliance. To activate the drawer 1, press '1' button. Press MANUAL mode. Adjust the temperature to 195°C and time for 5 minutes. Slide the drawer back into appliance and press the Start/Stop button to begin cooking. 7. Remove the drawer, shake, and cook for another 5 minutes, or until the okra is crisp. 8. When done, let cool before serving.

Crispy Salty Tofu

Prep Time: 5 minutes Cook: 15 minutes Serves: 4

25g chickpea flour
40g arrowroot (or cornstarch)
1 teaspoon sea salt
1 teaspoon granulated garlic
½ teaspoon freshly grated black pepper
1 (425g) package tofu, firm or extra-firm
Cooking oil spray (sunflower, safflower, or refined coconut)
Asian Spicy Sweet Sauce, optional

1. In a medium bowl, combine the flour, arrowroot, salt, garlic, and pepper. Stir well to combine. 2. Cut the tofu into cubes. Place the cubes into the flour mixture. Toss well to coat. Spray the tofu with oil and toss again. 3. Spray the drawer with the oil. Place the tofu in a single layer in the drawer and spray the tops with oil. You may have to do this in 2 batches, depending on the size of your appliance. 4. Press the Start/Stop button to switch on the appliance. To activate the drawer 1, press '1' button. Press MANUAL mode. Adjust the temperature to 200°C and time for 8 minutes. Slide the drawer back into appliance and press the Start/Stop button to begin cooking. 5. Remove the drawer and spray again with oil. Toss gently or turn the pieces over. Spray with oil again and fry for another 7 minutes, or until golden-browned and very crisp. 6. Serve immediately, either plain or with the Asian Spicy Sweet Sauce.

Air Fried Spiced Acorn Squash

Prep Time: 5 minutes **Cook: 15 minutes** **Serves: 2**

1 teaspoon coconut oil
1 medium acorn squash, halved crosswise and seeded
1 teaspoon light brown sugar
Few dashes of ground nutmeg
Few dashes of ground cinnamon

1. Rub the coconut oil on the cut sides of the squash. Sprinkle with the brown sugar, nutmeg, and cinnamon. 2. Arrange the squash halves, cut sides up, in the drawer. 3. Press the Start/Stop button to switch on the appliance. To activate the drawer 1, press '1' button. Press MANUAL mode. Adjust the temperature to 160°C and time for 15 minutes. 4. Slide the drawer back into appliance and press the Start/Stop button to begin cooking. Cook until soft in the centre when pierced with a paring knife. 5. Serve immediately.

Brussels Sprouts with Bacon

Prep Time: 10 minutes **Cook: 23 minutes** **Serves: 4**

3 slices centre-cut bacon, halved
455g Brussels sprouts, trimmed and halved
1½ tablespoons extra-virgin olive oil
¼ teaspoon kosher salt
¼ teaspoon dried thyme

1. Arrange the bacon in a single layer in the drawer. 2. Press the Start/Stop button to switch on the appliance. To activate the drawer 1, press '1' button. Press MANUAL mode. Adjust the temperature to 175°C and time for 10 minutes. Slide the drawer back into appliance and press the Start/Stop button to begin cooking. Cook for about 10 minutes, until crisp. 3. Transfer the bacon to a plate lined with paper towels to drain and then roughly chop. 4. In a large bowl, combine the Brussels sprouts with the oil. Sprinkle with the salt and thyme and toss well to coat. 5. Working in batches, arrange a single layer of the Brussels sprouts in the drawer. Slide the drawer back into appliance and press the Start/Stop button to begin cooking. Cook at 175°C for about 13 minutes, shaking halfway, until golden brown and tender. 6. Transfer to a serving dish, top with the bacon, and serve.

Bacon-Wrapped Asparagus

Prep Time: 10 minutes **Cook: 8-10 minutes** **Serves: 4**

20 asparagus spears (340g), tough ends trimmed
Olive oil spray
½ teaspoon grated lemon zest
⅛ teaspoon kosher salt
Freshly ground black pepper
4 slices centre-cut bacon

1. Place the asparagus on a small sheet pan and spritz with the olive oil. Season with the salt, lemon zest, and pepper to taste, tossing to coat. Group the asparagus into 4 bundles of 5 spears and wrap the centre of each bundle with a slice of bacon. 2. Place the asparagus bundles in the drawer. 3. Press the Start/Stop button to switch on the appliance. To activate the drawer 1, press '1' button. Press MANUAL mode. Adjust the temperature to 200°C and time for 8 minutes. 4. Slide the drawer back into appliance and press the Start/Stop button to begin cooking. Cook until the bacon is browned and the asparagus is slightly charred on the edges, 8 to 10 minutes, depending on the thickness of the spears. 5. Serve immediately.

Crispy Breaded Fried Aubergine

Prep Time: 10 minutes **Cook: 8 minutes** **Serves: 8**

1 large aubergine (about 680g)
¾ teaspoon kosher salt
Freshly ground black pepper
3 large eggs
150g seasoned bread crumbs, whole wheat or gluten-free
Olive oil spray
Marinara sauce, for dipping (optional)

1. Slice the ends off the aubergine and cut into ¼-inch-thick rounds, 40 to 42 slices. Season both sides with the salt and pepper to taste. 2. On a shallow plate, beat the eggs with 1 teaspoon water. Place the bread crumbs on another plate. Dredge each aubergine slice in the egg, then in the bread crumbs, pressing gently to adhere. Shake off any excess bread crumbs and arrange on a work surface. Generously spray both sides of the aubergine with oil. 3. Working in batches, arrange a single layer of the aubergine in the drawer. 4. Press the Start/Stop button to switch on the appliance. To activate the drawer 1, press '1' button. Press MANUAL mode. Adjust the temperature to 195°C and time for 8 minutes. 5. Slide the drawer back into appliance and press the Start/Stop button to begin cooking. Cook, flipping halfway, until crisp, golden, and cooked through in the centre. 6. Serve warm with the marinara, if desired.

Chapter 3 Snacks and Starters

Fried Green Tomatoes with Horseradish Drizzle

Prep Time: 18 minutes **Cook: 10-15 minutes** **Serves: 4**

2 eggs
60g buttermilk
65g cornmeal
45g breadcrumbs
¼ teaspoon salt
680g firm green tomatoes, cut in ¼-inch slices
Oil for misting or cooking spray

Horseradish Drizzle:

55g mayonnaise
55g sour cream
2 teaspoons prepared horseradish
½ teaspoon Worcestershire sauce
½ teaspoon lemon juice
⅛ teaspoon black pepper

1. Mix all ingredients for horseradish drizzle together and chill while you prepare the green tomatoes. 2. Beat the eggs and buttermilk together in a shallow bowl. 3. Mix the cornmeal, breadcrumbs, and salt together in a plate or shallow dish. 4. Dip 4 tomato slices in the egg mixture, then roll in the breadcrumb mixture. 5. Mist one side with oil and place in the drawer, oil-side down, in a single layer, and mist the top with oil. 6. Press the Start/Stop button to switch on the appliance. To activate the drawer 1, press '1' button. Press MANUAL mode. Adjust the temperature to 200°C and time for 10 minutes. 7. Slide the drawer back into appliance and press the Start/Stop button to begin cooking. Cook for 10 to 15 minutes, turning once, until brown and crispy. 8. Repeat steps 4 through 7 to cook remaining tomatoes. 9. Drizzle the horseradish sauce over tomatoes just before serving.

Fried Dill Pickles

Prep Time: 10 minutes **Cook: 11-15 minutes** **Serves: 4-6**

1 egg
1 tablespoon milk
¼ teaspoon hot sauce
500g sliced dill pickles, well drained
65g breadcrumbs
Oil for misting or cooking spray

1. Beat together the egg, milk, and hot sauce in a bowl large enough to hold all the pickles. 2. Add the pickles to the egg wash and stir well to coat. 3. Place the breadcrumbs in a large plastic bag or container with lid. 4. Drain the egg wash from pickles and place them in bag with the breadcrumbs. Shake to coat. 5. Pile the pickles into the drawer and spray with the oil. 6. Press the Start/Stop button to switch on the appliance. To activate the drawer 1, press '1' button. Press MANUAL mode. Adjust the temperature to 200°C and time for 5 minutes. Slide the drawer back into appliance and press the Start/Stop button to begin cooking. 7. Remove the drawer, shake, and spray with the oil. 8. Cook 5 more minutes. Shake and spray again. Separate any pickles that have stuck together and mist any spots you've missed. 9. Cook for 1 to 5 minutes longer or until dark golden brown and crispy. 10. When done, serve and enjoy.

Sausage Rolls

Prep Time: 5 minutes Cook: 5 minutes Serves: 6

For the Seasoning:
2 tablespoons sesame seeds
1½ teaspoons poppy seeds
1½ teaspoons dried minced onion
1 teaspoon salt
1 teaspoon dried minced garlic
For the Sausages:
1 (225g) package crescent roll dough
1 (340g) package mini smoked sausages (cocktail franks)

To make the seasoning: 1. In a small bowl, combine the sesame seeds, onion, salt, poppy seeds, and garlic and set aside.
To make the sausages: 1. Spray the drawer with the olive oil. 2. Remove the crescent dough from the package and lay it out on a cutting board. Separate the dough at the perforations. Cut each triangle of dough into fourths with a pizza cutter or sharp knife. 3. Drain the sausages and pat them dry with a paper towel. 4. Roll each sausage in a piece of dough. 5. Sprinkle the seasoning on top of each roll. 6. Place the seasoned sausage rolls into the greased drawer in a single layer. You will have to bake these in at least 2 batches. 7. Press the Start/Stop button to switch on the appliance. To activate the drawer 1, press '1' button. Press MANUAL mode. Adjust the temperature to 165°C and time for 5 minutes. 8. Slide the drawer back into appliance and press the Start/Stop button to begin cooking. 9. Using tongs, remove the sausages from the drawer and place them on a platter. 10. Repeat steps 6 through 9 with the second batch. 11. When done, serve and enjoy.

Mozzarella Sticks

Prep Time: 10 minutes Cook: 8 minutes Serves: 6

1 (12-count) package mozzarella sticks
1 (225g) package crescent roll dough
3 tablespoons unsalted butter, melted
15g panko bread crumbs
Marinara sauce, for dipping (optional)

1. Spray the drawer with the olive oil. 2. Cut each cheese stick into thirds. 3. Unroll the crescent roll dough. Cut the dough into 36 even pieces with a pizza cutter or sharp knife. 4. Wrap each small cheese stick in a piece of dough. Make sure that the dough is wrapped tightly around the cheese. Pinch the dough together at both ends, and pinch along the seam to ensure that the dough is completely sealed. 5. Using tongs, dip the wrapped cheese sticks in the melted butter, then dip the cheese sticks in the panko bread crumbs. 6. Place the cheese sticks in the greased drawer in a single layer. You may have to cook the cheese sticks in more than one batch. 7. Press the Start/Stop button to switch on the appliance. To activate the drawer 1, press '1' button. Press MANUAL mode. Adjust the temperature to 185°C and time for 5 minutes. 8. Slide the drawer back into appliance and press the Start/Stop button to begin cooking. 9. After 5 minutes, the tops should be golden brown. Using tongs, flip the cheese sticks and bake for another 3 minutes, or until golden brown on all sides. 10. Repeat until you use all of the dough. 11. Plate, serve with the marinara sauce (if you like), and enjoy!

Healthy Carrot Chips

Prep Time: 5 minutes Cook: 6-8 minutes Serves: 6

455g carrots, peeled and sliced ⅛ inch thick
2 tablespoons olive oil
1 teaspoon sea salt

1. In a large mixing bowl, combine the carrots, olive oil, and salt. Toss them together until the carrot slices are thoroughly coated with oil. 2. Place the carrot chips in the drawer in a single layer. You may have to bake the carrot chips in more than one batch. 3. Press the Start/Stop button to switch on the appliance. To activate the drawer 1, press '1' button. Press MANUAL mode. Adjust the temperature to 180°C and time for 3 minutes. 4. Slide the drawer back into appliance and press the Start/Stop button to begin cooking. 5. Remove the drawer and shake to redistribute the chips for even cooking. Continue to bake for 3 minutes more. 6. Check the carrot chips for doneness. If you like them extra crispy, give another shake and cook them for another 1 to 2 minutes. 7. When the chips are done, remove the drawer, pour the chips into a bowl, and serve.

Crispy Breaded Artichoke Hearts

Prep Time: 15 minutes Cook: 10 minutes Serves: 4-6

14 whole artichoke hearts packed in water
1 egg
60g all-purpose flour
15g panko bread crumbs
1 teaspoon Italian seasoning
Cooking oil

1. Squeeze excess water from the artichoke hearts and place them on paper towels to dry. 2. In a small bowl, beat the egg. In another small bowl, place the flour. In a third small bowl, add the bread crumbs and Italian seasoning, and stir. 3. Spray the drawer with the cooking oil. 4. Dip the artichoke hearts in the flour, then the egg, and then the bread crumb mixture. 5. Place the breaded artichoke hearts in the drawer. It is okay to stack them. Spray them with the cooking oil. 6. Press the Start/Stop button to switch on the appliance. To activate the drawer 1, press '1' button. Press MANUAL mode. Adjust the temperature to 195°C and time for 4 minutes. 7. Slide the drawer back into appliance and press the Start/Stop button to begin cooking. 8. Remove the drawer, flip the artichoke hearts, and continue to cook for another 4 minutes, or until the artichoke hearts have browned and are crisp. 9. When done, let cool before serving.

Garlic Sweet Potato Fries

Prep Time: 10 minutes **Cook: 25 minutes** **Serves: 4**

2 large sweet potatoes, peeled
1½ tablespoons cornstarch
1 tablespoon canola oil
1 tablespoon extra-virgin olive oil
1 teaspoon paprika
1 teaspoon garlic powder
Salt
Pepper

1. Cut the potatoes lengthwise to create fries. Place them in a large bowl with cold water and allow them to soak in the water for 1 hour. 2. Drain the sweet potatoes and pat dry with paper towels or napkins. 3. Place the fries in a sealable plastic bag and add the cornstarch. Seal the bag and shake to evenly coat the fries. 4. Place the fries in a large bowl and coat with the canola oil and olive oil. Add the paprika, salt, garlic powder, and pepper to taste. 5. Transfer the fries to the drawer. It is okay to stack the fries, but do not overcrowd the drawer. 6. Press the Start/Stop button to switch on the appliance. To activate the drawer 1, press '1' button. Press MANUAL mode. Adjust the temperature to 195°C and time for 10 minutes. 7. Slide the drawer back into appliance and press the Start/Stop button to begin cooking. 8. Remove the drawer, shake, and cook for an additional 10 to 15 minutes, until the fries are crisp. 9. When done, let cool before serving.

Buffalo Breaded Cauliflower Bites

Prep Time: 10 minutes **Cook: 25 minutes** **Serves: 4**

120 all-purpose flour
240ml water
1 teaspoon garlic powder
1 large head cauliflower, cut into florets (425g)
Cooking oil
85g Frank's RedHot Buffalo Wings sauce

1. In a large bowl, combine the flour, water, and garlic powder. Mix well. The mixture should resemble pancake batter. 2. Add the cauliflower to the batter and stir to coat. Transfer the cauliflower to another large bowl to drain the excess batter. 3. Spray the drawer with cooking oil and transfer the cauliflower to the drawer without stacking. You may cook in batches. Spray the cauliflower with cooking oil. 4. Press the Start/Stop button to switch on the appliance. To activate the drawer 1, press '1' button. Press MANUAL mode. Adjust the temperature to 185°C and time for 6 minutes. 5. Slide the drawer back into appliance and press the Start/Stop button to begin cooking. 6. Remove the drawer and transfer the cauliflower to a large bowl. Drizzle with the Buffalo sauce. Mix well. 7. Return the cauliflower to the drawer and cook for another 6 minutes, or until crisp. 8. Remove the cooked cauliflower from the drawer and then repeat to cook the remaining cauliflower. 9. When done, let cool before serving.

Chapter 4 Poultry

Southern Fried Chicken Drumsticks

Prep Time: 10 minutes Cook: 20 minutes Serves: 4

240ml buttermilk
2–3 sprigs fresh thyme
1 tablespoon lemon juice
1 teaspoon salt
8 chicken drumsticks, skin on
45g crushed pork rinds
2 teaspoons Old Bay seasoning

1. In a gallon-size resealable bag, combine the buttermilk, thyme, lemon juice, and salt. Add the drumsticks and massage the bag to ensure the chicken is thoroughly coated. Refrigerate for 2 hours. 2. In another gallon-size resealable bag, combine the pork rinds and Old Bay seasoning. Working with one or two drumsticks at a time, remove the chicken from the buttermilk mixture, discarding the marinade, and transfer to the bag with the pork rinds. Seal the bag and shake gently to coat the chicken. 3. Working in batches if necessary, arrange the drumsticks in the drawer, making sure they do not touch. 4. Press the Start/Stop button to switch on the appliance. To activate the drawer 1, press '1' button. Press MANUAL mode. Adjust the temperature to 180°C and time for 20 minutes. 5. Slide the drawer back into appliance and press the Start/Stop button to begin cooking. 6. Cook until the chicken skin is browned and a thermometer inserted into the thickest portion registers 75°C, pausing halfway through the cooking time to turn the chicken. 7. When done, serve and enjoy.

Chicken Cordon Bleu Casserole

Prep Time: 10 minutes Cook: 20-25 minutes Serves: 6

55g unsalted butter, softened
115g cream cheese, softened
1½ teaspoons Dijon mustard
2 tablespoons white wine vinegar
60ml water
450g shredded cooked chicken
115g ham, chopped
115g sliced Swiss or Provolone cheese

1. Lightly coat a casserole dish that will fits your appliance with olive oil and set aside. 2. In a large bowl, combine the butter, cream cheese, Dijon mustard, and vinegar with an electric mixer. With the motor running on low speed, slowly add the water and beat until smooth. Set aside. 3. Arrange an even layer of chicken in the bottom of the prepared dish, followed by the ham. Spread the butter and cream cheese mixture on top of the ham, followed by the cheese slices on the top layer. 4. Press the Start/Stop button to switch on the appliance. To activate the drawer 1, press '1' button. Press MANUAL mode. Adjust the temperature to 195°C and time for 20 minutes. 5. Place the dish in the drawer 1 and slide the drawer back into appliance. Press the Start/Stop button to begin cooking. Cook for 20 to 25 minutes until warmed through and the cheese has browned. 6. When done, serve and enjoy.

The Best Chicken Fajitas

Prep Time: 10 minutes **Cook: 14 minutes** **Serves: 4**

455g chicken breast tenders, chopped into bite-size pieces
½ onion, thinly sliced
½ red bell pepper, seeded and thinly sliced
½ green bell pepper, seeded and thinly sliced
1 tablespoon vegetable oil
1 tablespoon fajita seasoning
1 teaspoon kosher salt
Juice of ½ lime
8 large lettuce leaves
240g prepared guacamole

1. In a large bowl, combine the chicken, onion, and peppers. Drizzle with the vegetable oil and toss until thoroughly coated. Add the fajita seasoning and salt and toss again. 3. Working in batches if necessary, place the chicken and vegetables in a single layer in the drawer. 4. Press the Start/Stop button to switch on the appliance. To activate the drawer 1, press '1' button. Press MANUAL mode. Adjust the temperature to 200°C and time for 14 minutes. 5. Slide the drawer back into appliance and press the Start/Stop button to begin cooking. Cook until the vegetables are tender and a thermometer inserted into the thickest piece of chicken registers 75°C, pausing halfway through the cooking time to shake. 6. Transfer the mixture to a serving platter and drizzle with the fresh lime juice. Serve with the lettuce leaves and top with the guacamole.

Flavourful Cobb Salad

Prep Time: 10 minutes **Cook: 5 minutes** **Serves: 6**

8 slices reduced-sodium bacon
8 chicken breast tenders (about 680g)
335g chopped romaine lettuce
150g cherry tomatoes, halved
¼ red onion, thinly sliced
2 hard-boiled eggs, peeled and sliced

Avocado-Lime Dressing:

125g plain Greek yoghurt
60ml milk
½ avocado
Juice of ½ lime
3 scallions, coarsely chopped
1 clove garlic
2 tablespoons fresh cilantro
⅛ teaspoon ground cumin
Salt and freshly ground black pepper

1. Wrap a piece of bacon around each piece of chicken and secure with a toothpick. Working in batches if necessary, arrange the bacon-wrapped chicken in a single layer in the drawer. 2. Press the Start/Stop button to switch on the appliance. To activate the drawer 1, press '1' button. Press MANUAL mode. Adjust the temperature to 200°C and time for 8 minutes. 3. Slide the drawer back into appliance and press the Start/Stop button to begin cooking. Cook until the bacon is browned and a thermometer inserted into the thickest piece of chicken register 75°C. 4. Let cool for a few minutes and then slice into bite-size pieces. 5. Make the dressing by combining the yoghurt, milk, avocado, garlic, cilantro, lime juice, scallions, and cumin in a blender or food processor. Puree until smooth. Season to taste with the salt and freshly ground pepper. 4. To assemble the salad, in a large bowl, combine the lettuce, tomatoes, and onion. Drizzle the dressing over the vegetables and toss gently until thoroughly combined. Arrange the chicken and eggs on top just before serving.

Chicken and Broccoli Casserole

Prep Time: 10 minutes Cook: 20-25 minutes Serves: 4

220g broccoli, chopped into florets
450g shredded cooked chicken
115g cream cheese
75g heavy cream
1½ teaspoons Dijon mustard
½ teaspoon garlic powder
Salt and freshly ground black pepper
2 tablespoons chopped fresh basil
115g shredded Cheddar cheese

1. Lightly coat a casserole dish that will fits your appliance with olive oil and set aside. 2. Place the broccoli in a large glass bowl with 1 tablespoon of water and cover with a microwavable plate. Microwave on high for 2 to 3 minutes until the broccoli is bright green but not mushy. Drain if necessary and add to another large bowl along with the shredded chicken. 3. In the same glass bowl used to microwave the broccoli, combine the cream cheese and cream. Microwave for 30 seconds to 1 minute on high and stir until smooth. Add the mustard and garlic powder and season to taste with salt and freshly ground black pepper. Whisk until the sauce is smooth. 4. Pour the warm sauce over the broccoli and chicken mixture and then add the basil. Using a silicone spatula, gently fold the mixture until thoroughly combined. 5. Transfer the chicken mixture to the prepared casserole dish and top with the cheese. 6. Press the Start/Stop button to switch on the appliance. To activate the drawer 1, press '1' button. Press MANUAL mode. Adjust the temperature to 200°C and time for 20 minutes. 7. Place the dish in the drawer 1 and slide the drawer back into appliance. Press the Start/Stop button to begin cooking. Cook for 20 to 25 minutes until warmed through and the cheese has browned. 8. When done, serve and enjoy.

Spiced Turkey Breast

Prep Time: 5 minutes Cook: 45-55 minutes Serves: 10

1 tablespoon sea salt
1 teaspoon paprika
1 teaspoon onion powder
1 teaspoon garlic powder
½ teaspoon freshly ground black pepper
1820g bone-in, skin-on turkey breast
2 tablespoons unsalted butter, melted

1. In a small bowl, combine the salt, paprika, garlic powder, onion powder, and pepper. 2. Sprinkle the seasonings all over the turkey. Brush the turkey with some of the melted butter. 3. Place the turkey in the drawer, skin-side down. 4. Press the Start/Stop button to switch on the appliance. To activate the drawer 1, press '1' button. Press MANUAL mode. Adjust the temperature to 175°C and time for 25 minutes. 5. Slide the drawer back into appliance and press the Start/Stop button to begin cooking. 6. Flip the turkey and brush it with the remaining butter. Continue cooking for an additional 20 to 30 minutes, until an instant-read thermometer reads 70°C. 7. Remove the turkey breast from the drawer. Tent a piece of aluminium foil over the turkey and allow it to rest for about 5 minutes before serving.

Chicken Parmesan

Prep Time: 25 minutes **Cook: 18-20 minutes** **Serves: 8**

910g boneless, skinless chicken breasts or thighs
110g finely ground blanched almond flour
100g grated Parmesan cheese
1 teaspoon Italian seasoning
Sea salt
Freshly ground black pepper
2 large eggs
Avocado oil spray
85g sugar-free marinara sauce
115g fresh mozzarella cheese, sliced or shredded

1. Place the chicken in a zip-top bag or between two pieces of plastic wrap. Pound the chicken to a uniform ½-inch thickness with a meat mallet or heavy skillet. 2. Place the almond flour, Italian seasoning, Parmesan cheese, salt, and pepper to taste in a large shallow bowl. 3. In a separate shallow bowl, beat the eggs. 4. Dip a chicken breast in the egg, then coat it in the almond flour mixture, making sure to press the coating onto the chicken gently. Repeat with the remaining chicken. 5. Spray both sides of the chicken well with oil and place the pieces in a single layer in the drawer, working in batches if necessary. 6. Press the Start/Stop button to switch on the appliance. To activate the drawer 1, press '1' button. Press MANUAL mode. Adjust the temperature to 200°C and time for 10 minutes. 7. Slide the drawer back into appliance and press the Start/Stop button to begin cooking. 8. Flip the chicken with a spatula. Spray each piece with more oil and continue cooking for 5 minutes more. 9. Top each chicken piece with the marinara sauce and mozzarella. Return to the appliance and cook for 3 to 5 minutes, until the cheese is melted and an instant-read thermometer reads 70°C. 10. Let the chicken rest for 5 minutes, then serve.

Crispy Duck with Cherry Sauce

Prep Time: 10 minutes **Cook: 35-36 minutes** **Serves: 2-4**

1 whole duck (up to 2275g), split in half, back and rib bones removed
1 teaspoon olive oil
Salt and freshly ground black pepper

Cherry Sauce:

1 tablespoon butter
1 shallot, minced
120ml sherry
240g cherry preserves
240ml chicken stock
1 teaspoon white wine vinegar
1 teaspoon fresh thyme leaves
Salt and freshly ground black pepper

1. Trim some of the fat from the duck. Rub the olive oil on the duck and season with the salt and pepper. Place the duck halves in the drawer, breast side up and facing the centre of the drawer. 3. Press the Start/Stop button to switch on the appliance. To activate the drawer 1, press '1' button. Press MANUAL mode. Adjust the temperature to 200°C and time for 20 minutes. 4. Slide the drawer back into appliance and press the Start/Stop button to begin cooking. 5. Turn the duck over and cook for another 6 minutes. 6. While duck is cooking, make the cherry sauce. In a large sauté pan, melt the butter. Add the shallot and sauté until it is just starting to brown, 2 to 3 minutes. Add the sherry and deglaze the pan by scraping up any brown bits from the bottom of the pan. Simmer the liquid for a few minutes, until it has reduced by half. Add the cherry preserves, chicken stock, and white wine vinegar. Whisk well to combine all the ingredients. Simmer the sauce until it thickens and coats the back of a spoon, 5 to 7 minutes. Season with the salt and pepper and stir in the fresh thyme leaves. 7. Remove the drawer, spoon some cherry sauce over the duck, and continue to cook at 200°C for 4 more minutes. Then, turn the duck halves back over so that the breast side is facing up. Spoon more cherry sauce over the top of the duck, covering the skin completely. Cook for 3 more minutes and then remove the duck to a plate to rest for a few minutes. 8. Serve the duck in halves, or cut each piece in half again for a smaller serving. Spoon any additional sauce over the duck or serve it on the side.

Tortilla Crusted Chicken Breasts

Prep Time: 10 minutes **Cook: 12 minutes** **Serves: 2**

80g flour
1 teaspoon salt
1½ teaspoons chilli powder
1 teaspoon ground cumin
Freshly ground black pepper
1 egg, beaten
25g coarsely crushed yellow corn tortilla chips
2 (85g to 115g) boneless chicken breasts
Vegetable oil
130g salsa
60g crumbled queso fresco
Fresh cilantro leaves
Sour cream or guacamole (optional)

1. Set up a dredging station with three shallow dishes. Combine the flour, salt, cumin, chilli powder, and black pepper in the first shallow dish. Beat the egg in the second shallow dish. Place the crushed tortilla chips in the third shallow dish. 2. Dredge the chicken in the spiced flour, covering all sides of the breast. Then dip the chicken into the egg, coating the chicken completely. Finally, place the chicken into the tortilla chips and press the chips onto the chicken to make sure they adhere to all sides of the breast. Spray the coated chicken breasts on both sides with the vegetable oil. 3. Press the Start/Stop button to switch on the appliance. To activate the drawer 1, press '1' button. Press MANUAL mode. Adjust the temperature to 195°C and time for 6 minutes. 4. Place the chicken in the drawer 1 and slide the drawer back into appliance. Press the Start/Stop button to begin cooking. 5. Turn the chicken breasts over and cook for another 6 minutes. 6. When the chicken has finished cooking, serve each breast with a little salsa, the crumbled queso fresco and cilantro as the finishing touch. Serve some sour cream and/or guacamole at the table, if desired.

Jalapeño Popper Chicken Breasts

Prep Time: 10 minutes **Cook: 14-17 minutes** **Serves: 8**

910g boneless, skinless chicken breasts or thighs
Sea salt
Freshly ground black pepper
226g cream cheese, at room temperature
115g Cheddar cheese, shredded
2 jalapeños, seeded and diced
1 teaspoon minced garlic
Avocado oil spray

1. Place the chicken in a large zip-top bag or between two pieces of plastic wrap. Pound the chicken until it is about ¼-inch thick with a meat mallet or heavy skillet. Season both sides of the chicken with the salt and pepper. 2. In a medium bowl, combine the cream cheese, Cheddar cheese, jalapeños, and garlic. Divide the mixture among the chicken pieces. Roll up each piece from the long side, tucking in the ends as you go. Secure with toothpicks. 3. Spray the outside of the chicken with oil. Place the chicken in a single layer in the drawer, working in batches if necessary. 4. Press the Start/Stop button to switch on the appliance. To activate the drawer 1, press '1' button. Press MANUAL mode. Adjust the temperature to 175°C and time for 7 minutes. 5. Slide the drawer back into appliance and press the Start/Stop button to begin cooking. 6. Flip the chicken and cook for another 7 to 10 minutes, until an instant-read thermometer reads 70°C. 7. When done, serve and enjoy.

Parmesan Chicken Fingers

Prep Time: 10 minutes Cook: 9 minutes Serves: 2-4

60g flour
1 teaspoon salt
Freshly ground black pepper
2 eggs, beaten
15g seasoned panko breadcrumbs
75g grated parmesan cheese
8 chicken tenders (about 455g) or 2 to 3 boneless, skinless chicken breasts, cut into strips
Vegetable oil
Marinara sauce

1. Set up a dredging station. Combine the flour, salt, and pepper in a shallow dish. Add the beaten eggs in second shallow dish. Mix the panko breadcrumbs and Parmesan cheese in a third shallow dish. 2. Dredge the chicken tenders in the flour mixture, then dip into the egg, and finally place the chicken in the breadcrumb mixture. Press the coating onto both sides of the chicken tenders. Arrange the coated chicken tenders on a baking sheet until they are all coated. Spray both sides of the chicken fingers with the vegetable oil. 3. Transfer the chicken fingers to the drawer. 4. Press the Start/Stop button to switch on the appliance. To activate the drawer 1, press '1' button. Press MANUAL mode. Adjust the temperature to 180°C and time for 9 minutes. 5. Slide the drawer back into appliance and press the Start/Stop button to begin cooking. Turn the chicken over halfway through the cooking time. 6. Serve immediately with marinara sauce, honey-mustard, ketchup or your favourite dipping sauce.

Apricot Glazed Chicken Thighs

Prep Time: 10 minutes Cook: 22 minutes Serves: 2-4

4 bone-in chicken thighs (about 910g)
Olive oil
1 teaspoon salt
¼ teaspoon freshly ground black pepper
½ teaspoon onion powder
240g apricot preserves
1½ tablespoons Dijon mustard
½ teaspoon dried thyme
1 teaspoon soy sauce
Fresh thyme leaves, for garnish

1. Brush or spray both the drawer and the chicken with the olive oil. Combine the salt, pepper and onion powder and season both sides of the chicken with the spice mixture. 2. Place the seasoned chicken thighs, skin side down in the drawer. 3. Press the Start/Stop button to switch on the appliance. To activate the drawer 1, press '1' button. Press MANUAL mode. Adjust the temperature to 195°C and time for 10 minutes. 4. Slide the drawer back into appliance and press the Start/Stop button to begin cooking. 5. While chicken is cooking, make the glaze by combining the apricot preserves, thyme, Dijon mustard, and soy sauce in a small bowl. 6. Remove the drawer, spoon half of the apricot glaze over the chicken thighs, and cook for 2 minutes. 7. Then flip the chicken thighs over so that the skin side is facing up and cook for an additional 8 minutes. 8. Finally, spoon and spread the rest of the glaze evenly over the chicken thighs and cook for a final 2 minutes. 9. Transfer the chicken to a serving platter and sprinkle the fresh thyme leaves on top.

Curry Mustard Chicken Tenders

Prep Time: 10 minutes Cook: 15 minutes Serves: 4

6 tablespoons mayonnaise
2 tablespoons coarse-ground mustard
2 teaspoons honey (optional)
2 teaspoons curry powder
1 teaspoon kosher salt
1 teaspoon cayenne pepper
455g chicken tenders

1. In a large bowl, whisk together the mayonnaise, honey (if using), curry powder, mustard, salt, and cayenne. Transfer half of the mixture to a serving bowl to serve as a dipping sauce. Add the chicken tenders to the large bowl and toss and stir until well coated. 2. Place the tenders in the drawer. 3. Press the Start/Stop button to switch on the appliance. To activate the drawer 1, press '1' button. Press MANUAL mode. Adjust the temperature to 175°C and time for 15 minutes. 4. Slide the drawer back into appliance and press the Start/Stop button to begin cooking. 5. Use a meat thermometer to ensure the chicken has reached an internal temperature of 75°C. 6. Serve the chicken with the dipping sauce.

Turkey Breast with Cherry Glaze

Prep Time: 15 minutes Cook: 54 minutes Serves: 6-8

1 (2275g) turkey breast
2 teaspoons olive oil
1 teaspoon dried thyme
½ teaspoon dried sage
1 teaspoon salt
½ teaspoon freshly ground black pepper
160g cherry preserves
1 tablespoon chopped fresh thyme leaves
1 teaspoon soy sauce
Freshly ground black pepper

1. First, make sure your turkey breast fits into the drawer. 2. Brush the turkey breast all over with the olive oil. Combine the thyme, salt, sage, and pepper and rub the outside of the turkey breast with the spice mixture. 3. Transfer the seasoned turkey breast to the drawer, breast side up. 4. Press the Start/Stop button to switch on the appliance. To activate the drawer 1, press '1' button. Press MANUAL mode. Adjust the temperature to 175°C and time for 25 minutes. 5. Slide the drawer back into appliance and press the Start/Stop button to begin cooking. 6. Turn the turkey breast on its side and cook for an additional 12 minutes. Turn the turkey breast on the opposite side and cook for 12 more minutes. The internal temperature of the turkey breast should reach 75°C when fully cooked. 7. While the turkey is cooking, make the glaze by combining the cherry preserves, soy sauce, fresh thyme, and pepper in a small bowl. 8. When the cooking is finished, return the turkey breast to an upright position and brush the glaze all over the turkey. Cook for a final 5 minutes, until the skin is nicely browned and crispy. 9. Allow the turkey to rest, loosely tented with foil, for at least 5 minutes before slicing and serving.

Chapter 5 Fish and Seafood

Shrimp Kebabs

Prep Time: 10 minutes Cook: 7 minutes Serves: 2

18 medium shelled and deveined shrimp
1 medium courgette, cut into 1" cubes
½ medium red bell pepper, cut into 1"-thick squares
¼ medium red onion, cut into 1"-thick squares
1½ tablespoons coconut oil, melted
2 teaspoons chilli powder
½ teaspoon paprika
¼ teaspoon ground black pepper

1. Soak four bamboo skewers in water for 30 minutes. Place a shrimp on the skewer, then a courgette, a pepper, and an onion. Repeat until all ingredients are utilised. 2. Brush each kebab with the coconut oil. Sprinkle with the chilli powder, paprika, and black pepper. Place the kebabs into the drawer. 3. Press the Start/Stop button to switch on the appliance. To activate the drawer 1, press '1' button. Press MANUAL mode. Adjust the temperature to 200°C and time for 7 minutes. 4. Slide the drawer back into appliance and press the Start/Stop button to begin cooking. Cook until the veggies are tender the shrimp is fully cooked. 5. Flip the kebabs halfway through the cooking time. 6. When done, serve warm.

Crab Cakes with Lemon Aioli

Prep Time: 10 minutes Cook: 10 minutes Serves: 4

2 (225g) cans crabmeat, drained and picked over to remove any bits of shell
2 eggs
30g almond flour
3 tablespoons mayonnaise
1 tablespoon Dijon mustard
1 teaspoon Old Bay seasoning
1 tablespoon chopped fresh parsley
½ teaspoon salt

Lemon Aioli:

55g mayonnaise
2 teaspoons fresh lemon juice
1 teaspoon Dijon mustard
½ teaspoon garlic powder
½ teaspoon Old Bay seasoning

1. Line the drawer with parchment paper. 2. In a large bowl, combine the crabmeat, mayonnaise, eggs, Dijon mustard, almond flour, Old Bay seasoning, parsley, and salt. Use a silicone spatula to gently fold until thoroughly combined, taking care not to break up the crabmeat too much. 3. Form the crab mixture patties with an ice cream scoop. Place the patties in a single layer on the lined drawer and then press lightly with the bottom of the scoop to flatten the patties into a circle about ½ inch thick. 4. Press the Start/Stop button to switch on the appliance. To activate the drawer 1, press '1' button. Press MANUAL mode. Adjust the temperature to 175°C and time for 10 minutes. 5. Slide the drawer back into appliance and press the Start/Stop button to begin cooking. Cook until lightly browned, pausing halfway through the cooking time to turn the patties. 6. Make the lemon aioli by combining the Dijon mustard, mayonnaise, lemon juice, garlic powder, and Old Bay seasoning in a small bowl. Stir until thoroughly combined. 7. Serve the crab cakes topped with the aioli sauce.

Crispy Coconut Shrimp with Spicy Dipping Sauce

Prep Time: 10 minutes **Cook: 8 minutes** **Serves: 4**

1 (70g) bag pork rinds
175g unsweetened shredded coconut flakes
45g coconut flour
1 teaspoon onion powder
1 teaspoon garlic powder
2 eggs
680g large shrimp, peeled and deveined
½ teaspoon salt
¼ teaspoon freshly ground black pepper

Spicy Dipping Sauce:

110g mayonnaise
2 tablespoons sriracha
Zest and juice of ½ lime
1 clove garlic, minced

1. In a food processor fitted with a metal blade, add the pork rinds and coconut flakes. Pulse until the mixture resembles coarse crumbs. Transfer to a shallow bowl. 2. In another shallow bowl, add the coconut flour, garlic powder, onion powder, and mix until thoroughly combined. 3. In a third shallow bowl, whisk the eggs until slightly frothy. 4. In a large bowl, season the shrimp with the salt and pepper, tossing gently to coat. 5. Working a few pieces at a time, dredge the shrimp in the flour mixture, then the eggs, and finally, the pork rind crumb mixture. Place the shrimp on a baking sheet until ready to cook. 6. Working in batches if necessary, place the shrimp in a single layer in the drawer. 7. Press the Start/Stop button to switch on the appliance. To activate the drawer 1, press '1' button. Press MANUAL mode. Adjust the temperature to 200°C and time for 8 minutes. 8. Slide the drawer back into appliance and press the Start/Stop button to begin cooking. Cook until cooked through, pausing halfway through the cooking time to turn the shrimp. 9. Make the sauce by combining the mayonnaise, lime zest and juice, sriracha, and garlic in a small bowl. Whisk until thoroughly combined. 10. Serve the shrimp with sauce.

Lemony Butter Cod

Prep Time: 5 minutes **Cook: 8 minutes** **Serves: 2**

2 (115g) cod fillets
2 tablespoons salted butter, melted
1 teaspoon Old Bay seasoning
½ medium lemon, sliced

1. Place the cod fillets into a round baking dish that fits your appliance. Brush each fillet with the butter and sprinkle with the Old Bay seasoning. Lay two lemon slices on each fillet. Cover the dish with foil and place into the drawer. 2. Press the Start/Stop button to switch on the appliance. To activate the drawer 1, press '1' button. Press MANUAL mode. Adjust the temperature to 175°C and time for 8 minutes. 3. Slide the drawer back into appliance and press the Start/Stop button to begin cooking. Flip halfway through the cooking time. 4. When cooked, internal temperature should be at least 60°C. Serve warm.

Shrimp and Chorizo Kebabs

Prep Time: 10 minutes **Cook: 12-15 minutes** **Serves: 4**

680g large shrimp, peeled and deveined
1 large bell pepper, seeded and chopped into 1-inch pieces
2 tablespoons olive oil
1 teaspoon smoked paprika
¾ teaspoon salt
3 cloves garlic, minced
225g smoked chorizo, sliced into ½-inch rounds

1. In a large bowl, combine the shrimp, bell pepper, paprika, olive oil, salt, and garlic. Toss gently until thoroughly coated. 2. Thread the shrimp, peppers, and sausage onto the skewers, alternating ingredients as you go. 3. Press the Start/Stop button to switch on the appliance. To activate the drawer 1, press '1' button. Press MANUAL mode. Adjust the temperature to 200°C and time for 12 minutes. 4. Working in batches if necessary, lace the skewers in the drawer 1. 5. Slide the drawer back into appliance and press the Start/Stop button to begin cooking. Cook the skewers for 12 to 15 minutes, until the peppers are tender and the shrimp are cooked through, pausing halfway through the cooking time to turn the skewers. 6. When done, serve and enjoy.

Classic Fish and "Chips"

Prep Time: 10 minutes **Cook: 10 minutes** **Serves: 2-3**

120g flour
½ teaspoon paprika
¼ teaspoon ground white pepper (or freshly ground black pepper)
1 egg
55g mayonnaise
480g salt & vinegar kettle cooked potato chips, coarsely crushed
340g cod
Lemon wedges

Tartar Sauce:

220g mayonnaise
80g dill pickle relish
2 tablespoons capers, rinsed and chopped
1 tablespoon lemon juice
Dash cayenne pepper
Salt and freshly ground black pepper

1. Set up a dredging station. Combine the flour, paprika, and pepper in a shallow dish. Combine the egg and mayonnaise in a second shallow dish. Place the crushed potato chips in a third shallow dish. 2. Cut the cod into 6 pieces. Dredge each piece of fish in the flour, then dip it into the egg mixture and then place it into the crushed potato chips. Make sure all sides of the fish are covered and pat the chips gently onto the fish so they stick well. 3. Place the coated fish fillets into the drawer. 4. Press the Start/Stop button to switch on the appliance. To activate the drawer 1, press '1' button. Press MANUAL mode. Adjust the temperature to 185°C and time for 10 minutes. 5. Slide the drawer back into appliance and press the Start/Stop button to begin cooking. Gently turn the fish over halfway through the cooking time. 6. When the dish is cooking, make the tartar sauce by mixing all the ingredients together in a bowl. Season to taste with the salt and freshly ground black pepper. 7. When the cooking is finished, transfer the fish to a platter and serve with tartar sauce and lemon wedges.

Garlic Butter Shrimp

Prep Time: 10 minutes **Cook: 8-10 minutes** **Serves: 4**

455g fresh large shrimp, peeled and deveined
1 tablespoon avocado oil
2 teaspoons minced garlic, divided
½ teaspoon red pepper flakes
Sea salt
Freshly ground black pepper
2 tablespoons unsalted butter, melted
2 tablespoons chopped fresh parsley

1. Place the shrimp in a large bowl and toss with the avocado oil, 1 teaspoon of minced garlic, and red pepper flakes. Season with the salt and pepper. 2. Place the shrimp in a single layer in the drawer. 3. Press the Start/Stop button to switch on the appliance. To activate the drawer 1, press '1' button. Press MANUAL mode. Adjust the temperature to 175°C and time for 6 minutes. 4. Slide the drawer back into appliance and press the Start/Stop button to begin cooking. 5. Flip the shrimp and cook for 2 to 4 minutes more, until the internal temperature of the shrimp reaches 50°C. 6. While the shrimp are cooking, in a small saucepan over medium heat, melt the butter and stir in the remaining 1 teaspoon of garlic. 7. Transfer the cooked shrimp to a large bowl, add the garlic butter, and toss well. Top with the parsley and serve warm.

Sweet and Spicy Salmon

Prep Time: 5 minutes **Cook: 10-12 minutes** **Serves: 4**

110g sugar-free mayonnaise (homemade, or store-bought)
2 tablespoons brown sugar substitute, such as Sukrin Gold
2 teaspoons Dijon mustard
1 canned chipotle chilli in adobo sauce, diced
1 teaspoon adobo sauce (from the canned chipotle)
455g salmon fillets
Salt
Freshly ground black pepper

1. In a small food processor, combine the mayonnaise, brown sugar substitute, chipotle pepper, Dijon mustard, and adobo sauce. Process for 1 minute until everything is combined and the brown sugar substitute is no longer granular. 2. Season the salmon with the salt and pepper. Spread half of the sauce over the fish and reserve the remainder of the sauce for serving. 3. Press the Start/Stop button to switch on the appliance. To activate the drawer 1, press '1' button. Press MANUAL mode. Adjust the temperature to 200°C and time for 5 minutes. 4. Place the salmon in the drawer 1 and slide the drawer back into appliance. Press the Start/Stop button to begin cooking. 5. Flip the salmon and cook for 5 to 7 minutes more, until an instant-read thermometer reads 50°C (for medium-rare). 6. Serve warm with the remaining sauce.

Black Cod with Grapes, Fennel, Pecans, and Kale

Prep Time: 10 minutes **Cook: 15 minutes** **Serves: 2**

2 (170g to 225g) fillets of black cod (or sablefish)
Salt and freshly ground black pepper
Olive oil
100g grapes
1 small bulb fennel, sliced ¼-inch thick
60g pecans
65g shredded kale
2 teaspoons white balsamic vinegar or white wine vinegar
2 tablespoons extra virgin olive oil

1. Season the cod fillets with the salt and pepper and drizzle, brush or spray a little olive oil on top. 2. Toss the grapes, fennel and pecans in a bowl with a drizzle of olive oil and season with the salt and pepper. 3. Press the Start/Stop button to switch on the appliance. 4. To activate the drawer 1, press '1' button. Press MANUAL mode. Adjust the time for 10 minutes and the temperature to 200°C. Place the fish, presentation side up (skin side down) in the drawer 1. Slide the drawer back into the appliance. 5. To activate the drawer 2, press '2' button. Press MANUAL mode. Adjust the time for 5 minutes and the temperature to 200°C. Place the grapes, fennel and pecans in the drawer 2. Slide the drawer back into the appliance. 6. Press the SYNC button in order to get the two foods ready at the same time. Press the Start/Stop button to begin cooking. Shake the vegetables once during the cooking time. 7. Transfer the vegetables to a bowl with the kale. Dress the kale with the balsamic vinegar and olive oil, season to taste with the salt and pepper. Serve the cooked fish with vegetables.

Shrimp Spring Rolls

Prep Time: 10 minutes **Cook: 22 minutes** **Serves: 4**

Olive oil
2 teaspoon minced garlic
140g finely sliced cabbage
110g matchstick cut carrots
2 (115g) cans tiny shrimp, drained
4 teaspoons soy sauce
Salt
Freshly ground black pepper
16 square spring roll wrappers

1. Spray the drawer lightly with olive oil. 2. Spray a medium sauté pan with the olive oil. Add the garlic to the sauté pan and cook over medium heat until fragrant, 30 to 45 seconds. Add the cabbage and carrots and sauté until the vegetables are slightly tender, about 5 minutes. 3. Add the shrimp and soy sauce and season with the salt and pepper, then stir to combine. Sauté until the moisture has evaporated, 2 more minutes. Set aside to cool. 4. Arrange a spring roll wrapper on a work surface so it looks like a diamond. Place 1 tablespoon of the shrimp mixture on the lower end of the wrapper. 5. Roll the wrapper away from you halfway, then fold in the right and left sides, like an envelope. Continue to roll to the very end, using a little water to seal the edge. Repeat with the remaining wrappers and filling. 6. Place the spring rolls in the drawer in a single layer, leaving room between each roll. Lightly spray with the olive oil. You may need to cook them in batches. 7. Press the Start/Stop button to switch on the appliance. To activate the drawer 1, press '1' button. Press MANUAL mode. Adjust the temperature to 185°C and time for 5 minutes. 8. Slide the drawer back into appliance and press the Start/Stop button to begin cooking. 9. Turn the rolls over, lightly spray with olive oil, and cook until heated through and the rolls start to brown, 5 to 10 more minutes. 10. When done, serve and enjoy.

Lemon-Garlic Tilapia

Prep Time: 10 minutes **Cook: 15 minutes** **Serves: 4**

1 tablespoon lemon juice
1 tablespoon olive oil
1 teaspoon minced garlic
½ teaspoon chilli powder
4 (140g to 170g) tilapia fillets

1. Line the drawer with perforated air fryer liners. 2. In a large, shallow bowl, mix together the lemon juice, olive oil, garlic, and chilli powder to make a marinade. Place the tilapia fillets in the bowl and coat evenly. 3. Arrange the fillets in the drawer in a single layer, leaving space between each fillet. You may need to cook in more than one batch. 4. Press the Start/Stop button to switch on the appliance. To activate the drawer 1, press '1' button. Press MANUAL mode. Adjust the temperature to 195°C and time for 10 minutes. 5. Slide the drawer back into appliance and press the Start/Stop button to begin cooking. Cook until the fish is cooked and flakes easily with a fork, 10 to 15 minutes. 6. When done, serve and enjoy.

Cajun Fish Tacos

Prep Time: 10 minutes **Cook: 15 minutes** **Serves: 6**

2 teaspoons avocado oil
1 tablespoon Cajun seasoning
4 (140 to 170 g) tilapia fillets
1 (400g) package coleslaw mix
12 corn tortillas
2 limes, cut into wedges

1. Line the drawer with a perforated air fryer liner. 2. In a medium, shallow bowl, mix together the avocado oil and the Cajun seasoning to make a marinade. Add the tilapia fillets and coat evenly. 3. Place the fillets in the drawer in a single layer, leaving room between each fillet. You may need to cook in batches. 4. Press the Start/Stop button to switch on the appliance. To activate the drawer 1, press '1' button. Press MANUAL mode. Adjust the temperature to 195°C and time for 10 minutes. 5. Slide the drawer back into appliance and press the Start/Stop button to begin cooking. Cook until the fish is cooked and easily flakes with a fork, 10 to 15 minutes. 6. Assemble the tacos by placing some of the coleslaw mix in each tortilla. Add ⅓ of a tilapia fillet to each tortilla. Squeeze some lime juice over the top of each taco and serve.

Crispy Breaded Calamari

Olive oil
455g fresh calamari tubes, rinsed and patted dry
½ teaspoon salt, plus more as needed
½ teaspoon pepper, plus more as needed
120g whole-wheat flour
3 eggs
90g whole-wheat bread crumbs
2 teaspoons dried parsley

1. Spray the drawer lightly with the olive oil. 2. Cut the calamari into ¼-inch rings. Season them with the salt and black pepper. 3. In a shallow bowl, combine the whole-wheat flour, ½ teaspoon of salt, and ½ teaspoon of black pepper. 4. In a small bowl, whisk the eggs with 1 teaspoon of water. 5. In another shallow bowl, combine the bread crumbs and parsley. 6. Coat the calamari in the flour mixture, coat in the egg, and dredge in the bread crumbs to coat. 7. Place the calamari in the drawer in a single layer and spray the calamari lightly with the olive oil. You may need to cook the calamari in batches. 8. Press the Start/Stop button to switch on the appliance. To activate the drawer 1, press '1' button. Press MANUAL mode. Adjust the temperature to 195°C and time for 10 minutes. 9. Slide the drawer back into appliance and press the Start/Stop button to begin cooking. Cook until crispy and lightly browned, 10 to 15 minutes, shaking a few times during cooking to redistribute and evenly cook. 10. When done, serve and enjoy.

Red Snapper with Green Onions and Orange Salsa

Prep Time: 10 minutes Cook: 8 minutes Serves: 2

2 (140g to 170g) red snapper fillets
½ teaspoon Chinese five spice powder
Salt and freshly ground black pepper
Vegetable or olive oil, in a spray bottle
4 green onions, cut into lengths

Salsa:

2 oranges, peeled, segmented and chopped
1 tablespoon minced shallot
1 to 3 teaspoons minced red jalapeño or serrano pepper
1 tablespoon chopped fresh cilantro
Lime juice, to taste
Salt, to taste

1. Start by making the salsa. Cut the peel off the oranges, slicing around the oranges to expose the flesh. Segment the oranges by cutting in between the membranes of the orange. Chop the segments roughly and combine in a bowl with the shallot, Jalapeño or Serrano pepper, cilantro, lime juice and salt. Set the salsa aside. 2. Season the fish fillets with the five-spice powder, salt and freshly ground black pepper. Spray both sides of the fish fillets with oil. Toss the green onions with a little oil. 3. Transfer the fish to the drawer and scatter the green onions around the fish. 4. Press the Start/Stop button to switch on the appliance. To activate the drawer 1, press '1' button. Press MANUAL mode. Adjust the temperature to 200°C and time for 8 minutes. 5. Slide the drawer back into appliance and press the Start/Stop button to begin cooking. 6. Remove the fish from the drawer, along with the fried green onions. 7. Serve with the white rice and a spoonful of the salsa on top.

Chapter 6 Beef and Pork

Pork Chops with Caramelised Onions and Peppers

Prep Time: 20 minutes **Cook: 23-34 minutes** **Serves: 4**

4 bone-in pork chops (225g each)
1 to 2 tablespoons oil
2 tablespoons Cajun Seasoning, divided
1 yellow onion, thinly sliced
1 green bell pepper, thinly sliced
2 tablespoons light brown sugar

1. Spritz the pork chops with the oil. Sprinkle 1 tablespoon of Cajun Seasoning on one side of the chops. 2. Press the Start/Stop button to switch on the appliance. 3. To activate the drawer 1, press '1' button. Press MANUAL mode. Adjust the time for 4 minutes and the temperature to 200°C. Line the drawer 1 with parchment paper and spritz the parchment with oil. Place 2 pork chops, spice-side up, on the parchment. Slide the drawer back into the appliance. 4. To activate the drawer 2, press '2' button. Press MANUAL mode. Adjust the time for 4 minutes and the temperature to 200°C. Combine the onion, bell pepper, and brown sugar in the drawer 2, stirring until the vegetables are coated. Slide the drawer back into the appliance. 5. Press the SYNC button in order to get the two foods ready at the same time. Press the Start/Stop button to begin cooking. 6. Flip the chops, sprinkle with the remaining 1 tablespoon of Cajun Seasoning, and cook for 4 to 8 minutes more until the internal temperature reaches 60°C, depending on the chops' thickness. 7. Stir the vegetables. Cook for 3 to 6 minutes more to your desired doneness. 8. Spoon the vegetable mixture over the chops to serve.

Barbecue Pork Chops

Prep Time: 15 minutes **Cook: 10-12 minutes** **Serves: 4**

135g ketchup
2 tablespoons distilled white vinegar
2 tablespoons light brown sugar
1½ teaspoons salt
1½ teaspoons dry mustard
½ teaspoon chilli powder
4 bone-in pork chops (225g each)
1 to 2 tablespoons oil

1. In a medium bowl, whisk 240ml water, the ketchup, vinegar, salt, dry mustard, brown sugar, and chilli powder until blended. 2. Line the drawer with parchment paper and spritz it with oil. 3. Place the chops on the parchment and baste with the ketchup mixture. 4. Press the Start/Stop button to switch on the appliance. To activate the drawer 1, press '1' button. Press MANUAL mode. Adjust the temperature to 200°C and time for 4 minutes. 5. Slide the drawer back into appliance and press the Start/Stop button to begin cooking. 6. Flip the chops, spritz them with oil, baste again, and cook for 6 to 8 minutes more until the internal temperature reaches 60°C, depending on their thickness. 7. Serve with any extra sauce.

Barbecue Pulled Pork Sandwiches

Prep Time: 15 minutes Cook: 30 minutes Serves: 4

430g prepared barbecue sauce
2 tablespoons distilled white vinegar
2 tablespoons light brown sugar
1 tablespoon minced garlic
1 teaspoon hot sauce
910g pork shoulder roast
1 to 2 tablespoons oil
4 sandwich buns

1. In a medium bowl, stir together the barbecue sauce, brown sugar, vinegar, garlic, and hot sauce. 2. Line the drawer with parchment paper and spritz it with oil. 3. Place the pork on the parchment and baste it with a thick layer of sauce. 4. Press the Start/Stop button to switch on the appliance. To activate the drawer 1, press '1' button. Press MANUAL mode. Adjust the temperature to 180°C and time for 5 minutes. 5. Slide the drawer back into appliance and press the Start/Stop button to begin cooking. 6. Flip the pork and baste with sauce. Repeat 3 more times for a total of 20 minutes of cook time, ending with basting. 7. Increase the temperature to 200°C and cook the pork for 5 minutes. Flip, baste, and cook for 5 minutes more. Flip, baste, and let sit for 5 minutes before pulling the pork into 1-inch pieces. 8. Transfer to a bowl and toss the pork with the remaining sauce. Serve on buns.

Porcupine Meatballs

Prep Time: 10 minutes Cook: 32-34 minutes Serves: 4

125g instant rice
2 teaspoons salt, divided
1 tablespoon butter
455g ground beef (85% lean)
65g finely chopped onion
55g finely chopped green bell pepper
2 teaspoons garlic powder
1 teaspoon freshly ground black pepper
1 to 2 tablespoons oil

1. Mix 125g instant rice, 240ml water, 1 teaspoon salt, and butter in a pan that fits your appliance. 2. Press the Start/Stop button to switch on the appliance. To activate the drawer 1, press '1' button. Press MANUAL mode. Adjust the temperature to 175°C and time for 6 minutes. 3. Place the pan in the drawer 1 and slide the drawer back into appliance. Press the Start/Stop button to begin cooking. Cook the rice for 6 minutes. Stir and cook for 6 to 8 minutes more until done. 4. In a large bowl, mix the ground beef, cooked rice, green bell pepper, onion, garlic powder, the remaining 1 teaspoon of salt, and pepper. Shape the mixture into 20 (1-inch) meatballs. 5. Line the drawer with parchment paper. Place 10 meatballs on the parchment. 6. Press the Start/Stop button to switch on the appliance. To activate the drawer 1, press '1' button. Press MANUAL mode. Adjust the temperature to 175°C and time for 5 minutes. 7. Slide the drawer back into appliance and press the Start/Stop button to begin cooking. 8. Shake and spritz the meatballs with oil. Cook for 5 minutes more until browned and firm. 9. Remove the meatballs and keep warm. Repeat with the remaining meatballs. 10. When done, serve and enjoy.

Pork Milanese

Prep Time: 10 minutes Cook: 12 minutes Serves: 4

4 (1-inch) boneless pork chops
Fine sea salt and ground black pepper
2 large eggs
70g powdered Parmesan cheese (or pork dust for dairy-free)
Chopped fresh parsley, for garnish
Lemon slices, for serving

1. Spray the drawer with the avocado oil. 2. Place the pork chops between 2 sheets of plastic wrap and pound them with the flat side of a meat tenderiser until they're ¼ inch thick. Lightly season both sides of the chops with the salt and pepper. 3. Lightly beat the eggs in a shallow bowl. Divide the Parmesan cheese evenly between 2 bowls and set the bowls in this order: Parmesan, eggs, Parmesan. Dredge a chop in the first bowl of Parmesan, then dip it in the eggs, and then dredge it again in the second bowl of Parmesan, making sure both sides and all edges are well coated. Repeat with the remaining chops. 4. Press the Start/Stop button to switch on the appliance. To activate the drawer 1, press '1' button. Press MANUAL mode. Adjust the temperature to 200°C and time for 12 minutes. 5. Place the chops in the drawer 1 and slide the drawer back into appliance. Press the Start/Stop button to begin cooking. Cook until the internal temperature reaches 60°C, flipping halfway through. 6. Garnish with the fresh parsley and serve immediately with the lemon slices.

Southern-Style Cola Meat Loaf

Prep Time: 20 minutes Cook: 45 minutes Serves: 6

For the Glaze:
125g chilli sauce
120ml cola
1 tablespoon mustard
1 tablespoon cornstarch

For the Meat Loaf:
75g panko bread crumbs
1½ teaspoons Italian-Style Seasoning
1 teaspoon salt
½ teaspoon freshly ground black pepper
680g ground beef (85% lean)
50g minced onion
1 large egg
125g chilli sauce
120ml cola
2 tablespoons ketchup
1½ tablespoons mustard
1 to 2 tablespoons oil

To make the glaze: 1. In a small bowl, whisk the chilli sauce, cola, mustard, and cornstarch until blended. 2. Set aside, covered.
To make the meat loaf: 1. In a large bowl, stir together the bread crumbs, Italian-Style Seasoning, salt, and pepper. Add the ground beef, onion, cola, ketchup, egg, chilli sauce, and mustard. Mix until blended. 2. Spritz a pan that fits your appliance with oil. 3. Add the meat loaf mixture to the prepared pan. Cover with aluminium foil and place in the drawer. 4. Press the Start/Stop button to switch on the appliance. To activate the drawer 1, press '1' button. Press MANUAL mode. Adjust the temperature to 195°C and time for 20 minutes. 5. Slide the drawer back into appliance and press the Start/Stop button to begin cooking. 6. Uncover the meat loaf. Whisk the glaze and spread it over the meat loaf. Recover and cook for 25 minutes, more until the glaze has thickened and the meat loaf is no longer pink inside. 7. Brush with more glaze, if desired, and serve.

Hamburger Steak with Mushroom Gravy

Prep Time: 20 minutes Cook: 29-34 minutes Serves: 4

For the Mushroom Gravy:

1 (30g) envelope dry onion soup mix
45g cornstarch
230g diced or sliced mushrooms

For the Hamburger Steak:

455g ground beef (85% lean)
70g minced onion
65g Italian-style bread crumbs
2 teaspoons Worcestershire sauce
1 teaspoon salt
1 teaspoon freshly ground black pepper
1 to 2 tablespoons oil

1. In a bowl that fits your appliance, whisk the soup mix, cornstarch, mushrooms, and 480ml water until blended. 2. In a large bowl, mix the ground beef, onion, bread crumbs, Worcestershire sauce, salt, and pepper until blended. Shape the beef mixture into 4 patties. 3. Press the Start/Stop button to switch on the appliance. 4. To activate the drawer 1, press '1' button. Press MANUAL mode. Adjust the time for 7 minutes and the temperature to 160°C. Place the patties in the drawer 1. Slide the drawer back into the appliance. 5. To activate the drawer 2, press '2' button. Press MANUAL mode. Adjust the time for 10 minutes and the temperature to 175°C. Place the bowl in the drawer 2. Slide the drawer back into the appliance. 6. Press the SYNC button in order to get the two foods ready at the same time. Press the Start/Stop button to begin cooking. 7. Flip the patties, spritz them with oil, and cook for 7 minutes more, until the internal temperature reaches 60°C. 8. Stir the gravy and cook for 5 to 10 minutes more to your desired thickness. 9. When done, serve the steak with mushroom gravy.

Italian Sausages with Peppers and Onions

Prep Time: 5 minutes Cook: 28 minutes Serves: 3

1 medium onion, thinly sliced
1 yellow or orange bell pepper, thinly sliced
1 red bell pepper, thinly sliced
60ml avocado oil or melted coconut oil
1 teaspoon fine sea salt
6 Italian sausages
Dijon mustard, for serving (optional)

1. Place the onion and peppers in a large bowl. Drizzle with the oil and toss well to coat the veggies. Season with the salt. 2. Press the Start/Stop button to switch on the appliance. To activate the drawer 1, press '1' button. Press MANUAL mode. Adjust the temperature to 200°C and time for 8 minutes. 3. Place the onion and peppers in the drawer 1 and slide the drawer back into appliance. Press the Start/Stop button to begin cooking. 4. Stir halfway through. Remove from the drawer and set aside. 5. Spray the drawer with the avocado oil. Place the sausages in the drawer and cook for at 200°C for 20 minutes, or until crispy and golden brown. 6. During the last minute or two of cooking, add the onion and peppers to the drawer with the sausages to warm them through. 7. Place the onion and peppers on a serving platter and arrange the sausages on top. Serve Dijon mustard on the side, if desired.

Beef and Broccoli Stir-Fry

Prep Time: 10 minutes Cook: 20 minutes Serves: 2

230g sirloin steak, thinly sliced
2 tablespoons soy sauce (or liquid aminos)
¼ teaspoon grated ginger
¼ teaspoon finely minced garlic
1 tablespoon coconut oil
200g broccoli florets
¼ teaspoon crushed red pepper
⅛ teaspoon xanthan gum
½ teaspoon sesame seeds

1. To marinate the beef, place the beef into a large bowl or storage bag and add the soy sauce, garlic, ginger, and coconut oil. Allow to marinate for 1 hour in refrigerator. 2. Remove beef from marinade, reserving marinade, and place the beef into the drawer. 3. Press the Start/Stop button to switch on the appliance. To activate the drawer 1, press '1' button. Press MANUAL mode. Adjust the temperature to 160°C and time for 20 minutes. 4. Slide the drawer back into appliance and press the Start/Stop button to begin cooking. 5. After 10 minutes, add the broccoli and sprinkle the red pepper into the drawer and shake. 6. Pour the marinade into a skillet over medium heat and bring to a boil, then reduce to simmer. Stir in the xanthan gum and allow it to thicken. 7. When the cooking is finished, quickly empty the drawer into the skillet and toss. Sprinkle with the sesame seeds. Serve immediately.

Beef Empanadas

Prep Time: 15 minutes Cook: 10 minutes Serves: 4

455g 80/20 ground beef
60ml water
30g diced onion
2 teaspoons chilli powder
½ teaspoon garlic powder
¼ teaspoon cumin
170g shredded mozzarella cheese
55g blanched finely ground almond flour
55g full-fat cream cheese
1 large egg

1. In a medium skillet over medium heat, brown the ground beef for about 7 to 10 minutes. Drain the fat. Return the skillet to stove. 2. Add the water and onion to the skillet. Stir and sprinkle with the chilli powder, garlic powder, and cumin. Reduce the heat and simmer for another 3 to 5 minutes. Remove from heat and set aside. 3. In a large microwave-safe bowl, add the mozzarella, almond flour, and cream cheese. Microwave for 1 minute. Stir until smooth. Form the mixture into a ball. 4. Place dough between two sheets of parchment and roll out to ¼" thickness. Cut the dough into four squares. Place ¼ of ground beef onto the bottom half of each square. Fold the dough over and roll the edges up or press with a wet fork to close. 5. Crack the egg into a small bowl and whisk. Brush the egg over empanadas. 6. Cut a piece of parchment to fit the drawer, put the parchment in the drawer, and place the empanadas on the parchment. 7. Press the Start/Stop button to switch on the appliance. To activate the drawer 1, press '1' button. Press MANUAL mode. Adjust the temperature to 200°C and time for 10 minutes. 8. Slide the drawer back into appliance and press the Start/Stop button to begin cooking. 9. Flip the empanadas halfway through the cooking time. 10. Serve warm.

Parmesan-Crusted Steak

Prep Time: 7 minutes **Cook: 12 minutes** **Serves: 6**

115g (1 stick) unsalted butter, at room temperature
100g finely grated Parmesan cheese
30g finely ground blanched almond flour
680g New York strip steak
Sea salt
Freshly ground black pepper

1. Place the butter, Parmesan cheese, and almond flour in a food processor. Process until smooth. Transfer to a sheet of parchment paper and form into a log. Wrap tightly in plastic wrap. Freeze for 45 minutes or refrigerate for at least 4 hours. 2. While the butter is chilling, season the steak liberally with the salt and pepper. Let the steak rest at room temperature for about 45 minutes. 3. Press the Start/Stop button to switch on the appliance. To activate the drawer 1, press '1' button. Press MANUAL mode. Adjust the temperature to 200°C and time for 4 minutes. 4. Working in batches, if necessary, place the steak in the drawer 1 and slide the drawer back into appliance. Press the Start/Stop button to begin cooking. 5. Flip and cook for 3 minutes more, until the steak is brown on both sides. 6. Remove the steak from the drawer and arrange an equal amount of the Parmesan butter on top of each steak. Return the steak to the drawer and continue cooking for another 5 minutes, until an instant-read thermometer reads 50°C for medium-rare and the crust is golden brown, or to your desired doneness. 7. Transfer the cooked steak to a plate and let rest for 10 minutes before serving.

Greek Meatballs with Tzatziki Sauce

Prep Time: 10 minutes **Cook: 10-15 minutes** **Serves: 4**

455g 85% lean ground beef
125g grated courgette
65g crumbled feta cheese
2 tablespoons finely minced red onion
1 teaspoon garlic powder
1 teaspoon dried oregano
1 teaspoon salt
½ teaspoon freshly ground black pepper
2 teaspoons fresh lemon juice

Tzatziki Sauce:

115g sour cream
30g grated cucumber
1 tablespoon fresh lemon juice
½ teaspoon garlic powder
½ teaspoon dried dill
½ teaspoon salt
½ teaspoon freshly ground black pepper

1. In a large mixing bowl, combine the beef, red onion, garlic powder, courgette, feta, oregano, salt, black pepper, and lemon juice. Mix gently until thoroughly combined. Shape the mixture into 1¼-inch meatballs. 2. Working in batches if necessary, arrange the meatballs in a single layer in the drawer and coat lightly with the olive oil spray. 3. Press the Start/Stop button to switch on the appliance. To activate the drawer 1, press '1' button. Press MANUAL mode. Adjust the temperature to 175°C and time for 10 minutes. 4. Slide the drawer back into appliance and press the Start/Stop button to begin cooking. Cook for 10 to 15 minutes, until the meatballs are browned and a thermometer inserted into the centre of a meatball registers 70°C. 5. Pause halfway through the cooking time to shake the drawer. 6. Make the tzatziki sauce by combining the sour cream, cucumber, dill, salt, lemon juice, garlic powder, and black pepper in a bowl. Stir until thoroughly combined. 7. Serve the meatballs with tzatziki sauce.

Thai Beef Satay with Peanut Sauce

Prep Time: 10 minutes **Cook: 2-3 minutes** **Serves: 4**

Juice of 3 limes
10g fresh cilantro
4 cloves garlic
1-inch piece fresh ginger, peeled and chopped
2 tablespoons Swerve sugar replacement
2 tablespoons fish sauce
2 tablespoons reduced-sodium soy sauce
1 teaspoon sriracha or chilli-garlic sauce
2 teaspoons sesame oil
680g flank steak, sliced ¼ inch thick against the grain
2 medium cucumbers, peeled and sliced

Peanut Sauce:

130g creamy peanut butter
Juice of ½ lime
1 tablespoon reduced-sodium soy sauce
1 teaspoon Swerve sugar replacement
1 teaspoon grated fresh ginger
1 teaspoon chilli -garlic sauce
80ml water

1. In a food processor or blender, puree the lime juice, ginger, Swerve, fish sauce, cilantro, garlic, soy sauce, sriracha, and sesame oil. 2. Place the steak slices into a gallon-size resealable bag and add the marinade over the top of the meat. Seal the bag and refrigerate for at least an hour or up to 4 hours. 3. Make the peanut sauce by combining the peanut butter, soy sauce, Swerve, lime juice, ginger, and chilli-garlic sauce in a medium bowl. Slowly add the water and whisk until smooth. Cover and refrigerate until ready to serve. 4. Discard the marinade and thread the meat slices back and forth onto skewers. 5. Press the Start/Stop button to switch on the appliance. To activate the drawer 1, press '1' button. Press MANUAL mode. Adjust the temperature to 200°C and time for 2 minutes. 6. Working in batches if necessary, place the satay skewers in the drawer 1 and slide the drawer back into appliance. Press the Start/Stop button to begin cooking. Cook for 2 or 3 minutes until cooked through, pausing halfway through the time to turn the skewers. 7. Serve with the peanut sauce and the cucumbers.

London Broil with Herb Butter

Prep Time: 10 minutes **Cook: 20-25 minutes** **Serves: 4**

680g London broil top round steak
60ml olive oil
2 tablespoons balsamic vinegar
1 tablespoon Worcestershire sauce
4 cloves garlic, minced

Herb Butter:

6 tablespoons unsalted butter, softened
1 tablespoon chopped fresh parsley
¼ teaspoon salt
¼ teaspoon dried ground rosemary or thyme
¼ teaspoon garlic powder
Pinch of red pepper flakes

1. Place the beef in a gallon-size resealable bag. In a small bowl, stir together the olive oil, Worcestershire sauce, balsamic vinegar, and garlic. Pour the marinade over the beef, massaging gently to coat, and seal the bag. Let sit at room temperature for an hour or refrigerate overnight. 2. Make the herb butter by mixing the butter with the parsley, rosemary, salt, garlic powder, and red pepper flakes in a small bowl until smooth. Cover and refrigerate until ready to use. 3. Remove the beef from the marinade, discard the marinade, and place the beef in the drawer. 4. Press the Start/Stop button to switch on the appliance. To activate the drawer 1, press '1' button. Press MANUAL mode. Adjust the temperature to 200°C and time for 20 minutes. 5. Slide the drawer back into appliance and press the Start/Stop button to begin cooking. Cook for 20 to 25 minutes, until a thermometer inserted into the thickest part indicates the desired doneness, 50°C (rare) to 65°C (medium). 6. Pause halfway through the cooking time to turn the meat. 7. Let the beef rest for 10 minutes before slicing. Serve topped with the herb butter.

Roast Beef with Horseradish Cream

Prep Time: 10 minutes **Cook: 35-45 minutes** **Serves: 6**

910g beef roast top round or eye of round
1 tablespoon salt
2 teaspoons garlic powder
1 teaspoon freshly ground black pepper
1 teaspoon dried thyme

Horseradish Cream:

75g heavy cream
75g sour cream
80g prepared horseradish
2 teaspoons fresh lemon juice
Salt and freshly ground black pepper

1. Season the beef with the salt, garlic powder, black pepper, and thyme. Place the beef fat-side down in the drawer and lightly coat with the olive oil. 2. Press the Start/Stop button to switch on the appliance. To activate the drawer 1, press '1' button. Press MANUAL mode. Adjust the temperature to 200°C and time for 35 minutes. 3. Slide the drawer back into appliance and press the Start/Stop button to begin cooking. Cook for 35 to 45 minutes, until a thermometer inserted into the thickest part indicates the desired doneness, 50°C (rare) to 65°C (medium). 4. Pause halfway through the cooking time to turn the meat. 5. Let the beef rest for 10 minutes before slicing. 6. Make the horseradish cream by combining the heavy cream, horseradish, sour cream, and lemon juice in a small bowl. Whisk until thoroughly combined. Season to taste with salt and freshly ground black pepper. 7. Serve the beef with horseradish cream.

Poblano Pepper Cheeseburgers

Prep Time: 10 minutes **Cook: 31 minutes** **Serves: 4**

2 poblano chilli peppers
680g 85% lean ground beef
1 clove garlic, minced
1 teaspoon salt
½ teaspoon freshly ground black pepper
4 slices Cheddar cheese (about 85g)
4 large lettuce leaves

1. In a large bowl, combine the ground beef with the garlic, salt, and pepper. Shape the beef into 4 patties. 2. Press the Start/Stop button to switch on the appliance. 3. To activate the drawer 1, press '1' button. Press MANUAL mode. Adjust the time for 10 minutes and the temperature to 180°C. Place the patties in the drawer 1. Slide the drawer back into the appliance. 4. To activate the drawer 2, press '2' button. Press MANUAL mode. Adjust the time for 20 minutes and the temperature to 200°C. Place the poblano peppers in the drawer 2. Slide the drawer back into the appliance. 5. Press the SYNC button in order to get the two foods ready at the same time. Press the Start/Stop button to begin cooking. 6. Cook the burgers until a thermometer inserted into the thickest part registers 70°C, pausing halfway through the cooking time to turn the burgers. Cook the peppers until they are softened and beginning to char, pausing halfway through the cooking time to turn the peppers. 7. Top the burgers with the cheese slices and continue baking for a minute or two, just until the cheese has melted. 8. Transfer the peppers to a large bowl and cover with a plate. When cool enough to handle, peel off the skin, remove the seeds and stems, and slice into strips. Set aside. 9. Serve the burgers on a lettuce leaf topped with the roasted poblano peppers.

Chapter 7 Desserts

Baked Apples

Prep Time: 10 minutes **Cook: 20-25 minutes** **Serves: 4**

40g rolled oats
1 teaspoon brown sugar
1 tablespoon nondairy butter, softened
1 tablespoon coarsely chopped pecans
1 teaspoon ground cinnamon
4 large Granny Smith or other baking apples, cored

1. In a small bowl, combine the oats, butter, pecans, brown sugar, and cinnamon. 2. Using a small spoon, fill the apples with the oat mixture. 3. Press the Start/Stop button to switch on the appliance. To activate the drawer 1, press '1' button. Press MANUAL mode. Adjust the temperature to 180°C and time for 20 minutes. 4. Place the apples in the drawer 1 and slide the drawer back into appliance. Press the Start/Stop button to begin cooking. Cook for 20 to 25 minutes. 5. When done, serve and enjoy.

Sweet Caramelised Mixed Nut

Prep Time: 10 minutes **Cook: 7 minutes** **Serves: 3-4**

1 teaspoon sugar
1 teaspoon light agave syrup
1 teaspoon nondairy butter
60g coarsely chopped walnuts
60g coarsely chopped pecans
75g coarsely chopped dried apricots, cherries, cranberries, or raisins
¼ teaspoon ground cinnamon

1. Combine the sugar, agave syrup, and butter in a baking pan. 2. Press the Start/Stop button to switch on the appliance. To activate the drawer 1, press '1' button. Press MANUAL mode. Adjust the temperature to 180°C and time for 2 minutes. 3. Place the pan in the drawer 1 and slide the drawer back into appliance. Press the Start/Stop button to begin cooking. 4. Remove the pan from the drawer and add the walnuts, pecans, apricots, and cinnamon. Toss to coat. Return the pan to the drawer and cook at 200°C for 5 minutes, stirring at 3 minutes. 5. When done, serve and enjoy.

Apple Pie Taquitos

Prep Time: 5 minutes **Cook: 5 minutes** **Serves: 2**

2 to 3 spritzes canola oil
2 (6-inch) corn tortillas
1 teaspoon ground cinnamon, divided
60g apple pie filling

1. Spritz the drawer with the oil. 2. Spread 2 tablespoons pie filling onto 1 tortilla. Roll the tortilla up and place it in the drawer. Repeat this process to create the second taquito. Spritz more oil on the top of the tortillas. Sprinkle ½ teaspoon of the cinnamon over the taquitos. 3. Press the Start/Stop button to switch on the appliance. To activate the drawer 1, press '1' button. Press MANUAL mode. Adjust the temperature to 200°C and time for 4 minutes. 4. Slide the drawer back into appliance and press the Start/Stop button to begin cooking. 5. Turn the taquitos over, sprinkle the remaining ½ teaspoon cinnamon over the taquitos and cook for 1 minute longer. 6. When done, serve and enjoy.

Shortbread Cake

Prep Time: 5 minutes **Cook: 15-17 minutes** **Serves: 4**

225g nondairy butter
1 tablespoon vanilla extract
240g unbleached all-purpose flour, sifted
40 powdered sugar, sifted and packed, plus more as needed
120g finely chopped pecans

1. Cream the butter with a stand mixer fitted with the plastic paddle. Add the vanilla and continue mixing. Slowly add the flour, and then the powdered sugar, and mix well. Mix in the pecans. 2. Roll the dough into a ball. Press the dough into the bottom of a springform pan that fits your appliance (you may have to adjust how many cakes you make with the dough, based on the size of your appliance). 3. Press the Start/Stop button to switch on the appliance. To activate the drawer 1, press '1' button. Press MANUAL mode. Adjust the temperature to 165°C and time for 15 minutes. 4. Place the pan in the drawer 1 and slide the drawer back into appliance. Press the Start/Stop button to begin cooking. Cook for 15 to 17 minutes. 5. Transfer the pan to a baking rack and let the cake cool for 20 to 30 minutes. Serve the cake warm with sweet caramelised mixed nut or simply dust it with additional powdered sugar.

Blueberry Cake

Prep Time: 10 minutes Cook: 20 minutes Serves: 2

50g whole wheat pastry flour (or use a gluten-free baking blend)
3 tbsp (35g) raw or coconut sugar (or sweetener of choice, to taste)
1 tbsp (10g) ground flax seed
½ tsp baking powder
¼ tsp salt

Wet Ingredients:

70g fresh or thawed frozen blueberries
55g unsweetened vegan yoghurt (use a nut- or coconut-based yoghurt)
3 tbsp (45ml) unsweetened nondairy milk
½ tsp vanilla or lemon extract, your choice

1. Mix the dry ingredients together in a bowl. Then mix the wet ingredients in a large measuring cup. Add the wet to the dry and mix well. 2. Either spray some oil on a round cake or pie pan (or a loaf pan that fits in your appliance), or line the pan with parchment paper to keep it completely oil-free. 3. Press the Start/Stop button to switch on the appliance. To activate the drawer 1, press '1' button. Press MANUAL mode. Adjust the temperature to 175°C and time for 20 minutes. 4. Place the pan in the drawer 1 and slide the drawer back into appliance. Press the Start/Stop button to begin cooking. 5. If the middle is not well set or a knife doesn't come out clean when stuck in the middle, cook for 10 minutes more, depending on the size pan and your particular appliance. 6. When done, serve and enjoy.

Carrot Cake in a Mug

Prep Time: 10 minutes Cook: 15 minutes Serves: 1

25g whole wheat pastry flour
1 tbsp (15g) coconut or brown sugar, or sweetener of choice to taste
¼ tsp baking powder
¼ tsp ground cinnamon
⅛ tsp ground dried ginger
Pinch allspice
Pinch salt
2 tbsp (15ml) plus 2 tsp (5ml) unsweetened nondairy milk
2 tbsp (10g) grated carrot
2 tbsp (15g) chopped walnuts
1 tbsp (10g) raisins or chopped dates
2 tsp (10ml) mild oil

1. Oil an oven-safe mug. 2. Add the flour, sugar, cinnamon, ginger, baking powder, allspice and salt to a mixing bowl, then mix well with a fork. It's important to mix well so that the baking powder is evenly distributed. 3. Next add the milk, carrot, walnuts, raisins and oil, then mix again. 4. Press the Start/Stop button to switch on the appliance. To activate the drawer 1, press '1' button. Press MANUAL mode. Adjust the temperature to 175°C and time for 15 minutes. 5. Place the mug in the drawer 1 and slide the drawer back into appliance. Press the Start/Stop button to begin cooking. 6. Check with a fork to make sure the middle is cooked. If not, cook 5 minutes more. 7. When done, serve and enjoy.

Small Batch Brownies

⏰ Prep Time: 10 minutes 🍲 Cook: 20 minutes 🍽 Serves: 4

Dry Ingredients:

50g whole wheat pastry flour (use gluten-free baking blend)
100g vegan sugar (or sweetener of choice, to taste)
20g cocoa powder
1 tbsp (5g ground flax seeds)
¼ tsp salt

Wet Ingredients:

60ml nondairy milk
60ml aquafaba
½ tsp vanilla extract

Mix-Ins:

About 35g of any one or a combination of the following: chopped walnuts, hazelnuts, pecans, mini vegan chocolate chips, shredded coconut

1. Mix the dry ingredients together in a bowl. Mix the wet ingredients in a large measuring cup. Add the wet to the dry and mix well. 2. Add in the mix-in(s) of your choice and mix again. 3. Either spray some oil on a round cake or pie pan (or a loaf pan that fits your appliance), or line the pan with parchment paper to keep it completely oil-free. 4. Press the Start/Stop button to switch on the appliance. To activate the drawer 1, press '1' button. Press MANUAL mode. Adjust the temperature to 175°C and time for 20 minutes. 5. Place the filled pan in the drawer 1 and slide the drawer back into appliance. Press the Start/Stop button to begin cooking. 6. If the middle is not well set or a knife doesn't come out clean when stuck in the middle, cook for 5 minutes more and repeat as needed, depending on the size pan and your particular appliance. 7. When done, serve and enjoy.

Grilled Peanut Butter S'Mores Sandwiches

⏰ Prep Time: 5 minutes 🍲 Cook: 8-10 minutes 🍽 Serves: 2

2–4 tbsp (30–65g) peanut butter
4 slices bread (use gluten-free)
2–4 tbsp (5–10g) vegan mini marshmallows (or chopped large ones)
2–4 tbsp (30–60g) vegan mini chocolate chips
Spray oil, optional (omit)

1. Spread the peanut butter on one side of each of the 4 slices of bread. Sprinkle the marshmallows and chocolate chips over 2 of the slices and then top with the other peanut butter slices facedown. 2. Place one or more at a time into the drawer depending on the size you have. You can spray the top of the sandwich if you want to use oil. 3. Press the Start/Stop button to switch on the appliance. To activate the drawer 1, press '1' button. Press MANUAL mode. Adjust the temperature to 165°C and time for 5 minutes. 4. Slide the drawer back into appliance and press the Start/Stop button to begin cooking. 5. Flip, spray more oil, if using, and cook 3 to 5 minutes more, until the chocolate and the marshmallows get gooey. 6. When done, serve and enjoy.

Banana Spring Rolls

Prep Time: 10 minutes **Cook: 9 minutes** **Serves: 4**

1 medium (200g) ripe banana
8 vegan spring roll wrappers
2–4 tsp (5–10g) coconut sugar, or sweetener of choice to taste

1. Set up a space to assemble your spring rolls. I use a cutting board and set a small bowl of water in the corner. Slice the banana in half, then each half into 4 length-wise pieces (so they are in stick-like form). 2. Place a spring roll wrapper on the cutting board with a corner pointed toward you and another pointed toward the top of the cutting board. Place ¼ to ½ teaspoon sugar in the middle and spread it out to make a thick line, then place the banana piece on top of the sugar. 3. Fold the bottom point over the banana, about three fourths of the way up. Then fold the left corner to the centre, then the right to make an envelope shape. Continue rolling it up, dip your finger in the water and wet the edges of the top corner, then finish rolling and press to seal. 4. Repeat until all the spring rolls are wrapped. 5. Press the Start/Stop button to switch on the appliance. To activate the drawer 1, press '1' button. Press MANUAL mode. Adjust the temperature to 200°C and time for 5 minutes. 6. Place 4 to 8 spring rolls in the drawer 1 and If you want to, you can spritz the spring rolls with oil. Slide the drawer back into appliance and press the Start/Stop button to begin cooking. 7. Flip each one over with tongs and continue to cook for an additional 4 minutes. If you are using oil, spritz the spring rolls with oil on the side that's facing up now. 8. When done, serve and enjoy.

Savoury Pear Pecan Crostata

Prep Time: 15 minutes **Cook: 24 minutes** **Serves: 4**

2 ripe pears, peeled, cored, chopped or sliced
80g coarsely chopped pecans
2 tablespoons granulated sugar
1 tablespoon all-purpose flour
1 (11-inch) round pie crust
\

1. In a medium bowl, combine the pears and pecans. Sprinkle with the sugar and flour and toss gently to coat. 2. Ease the pie crust into a springform pan that fits your appliance. Press the crust down onto the bottom of the pan and up the sides. 3. Spoon the pear filling into the crust, spreading it evenly. 4. Gently pull the sides of the crust down over the filling, pleating the crust as you work, leaving the centre of the filling uncovered. 5. Using a foil sling, lower the springform pan into the drawer. 6. Press the Start/Stop button to switch on the appliance. To activate the drawer 1, press '1' button. Press MANUAL mode. Adjust the temperature to 175°C and time for 18 minutes. 7. Slide the drawer back into appliance and press the Start/Stop button to begin cooking. Cook for 18 to 24 minutes or until the pears are tender and bubbling slightly, and the crust is light golden brown. 8. Using the foil sling, remove the pan from the drawer and let cool on a wire rack for about 20 minutes. Remove the sides of the pan and slice the crostata into wedges to serve.

White Chocolate Blondies

Prep Time: 15 minutes **Cook: 20 minutes** **Serves: 6**

105g white chocolate chips
75g butter
45g brown sugar
50g granulated sugar
1 large egg
1 large egg yolk
1 teaspoon vanilla
120g all-purpose flour
⅛ teaspoon sea salt
Unsalted butter, at room temperature
55g semisweet chocolate chips

1. In a small saucepan over low heat, melt the white chocolate chips and butter together, stirring frequently until melted and combined, 4 to 5 minutes. 2. Transfer the mixture to a medium bowl. Add the brown and granulated sugars and beat well. Then add the egg, egg yolk, and vanilla and beat until smooth. 3. Stir in the flour and salt until just combined. 4. Grease a springform pan that fits your appliance with the unsalted butter. Add the batter to the pan and smooth the top. 5. Press the Start/Stop button to switch on the appliance. To activate the drawer 1, press '1' button. Press MANUAL mode. Adjust the temperature to 160°C and time for 15 minutes. 6. Place the pan in the drawer 1 and slide the drawer back into appliance. Press the Start/Stop button to begin cooking. Cook for 15 to 20 minutes, or until a toothpick inserted near the centre of the brownies comes out with only a few moist crumbs. 7. Remove the pan and let cool completely on a wire rack. 8. Melt the dark chocolate chips as directed on the package and drizzle on top of brownies.

Pistachio Baked Pears

Prep Time: 10 minutes **Cook: 14 minutes** **Serves: 4**

2 large ripe pears (Bosc or Anjou)
2 tablespoons butter, melted
3 tablespoons brown sugar
⅛ teaspoon cinnamon
110g whole unsalted shelled pistachios
Pinch sea salt

1. Cut the pears in half lengthwise, leaving the stems on one half of each pear. Carefully remove the seeds using a melon baller or spoon. 2. Put the pears into the drawer, cut-side up. Brush the pears with the melted butter and then sprinkle with the brown sugar and cinnamon. 3. Press the Start/Stop button to switch on the appliance. To activate the drawer 1, press '1' button. Press MANUAL mode. Adjust the temperature to 175°C and time for 8 minutes. 4. Slide the drawer back into appliance and press the Start/Stop button to begin cooking. 5. Remove the drawer and sprinkle the pears with the pistachios, concentrating them in the hollow where the seeds were. Sprinkle with the salt. 6. Return the drawer to the appliance and continue to cook for another 3 to 6 minutes or until the pears are tender and glazed. 7. When done, serve and enjoy.

Conclusion

The UK Tefal Dual Easy Fry & Grill Cookbook is a comprehensive guide designed to maximise the potential of your Tefal appliance, offering a wide range of recipes that cater to every taste and occasion. Whether you're preparing a quick weeknight dinner or a feast for friends and family, this cookbook simplifies the cooking process while ensuring that every dish is flavourful and satisfying.

With its focus on utilising both the air frying and grilling functions, the cookbook offers creative solutions for healthier meals without compromising on taste. From crispy chips to perfectly grilled meats and vegetables, each recipe is thoughtfully crafted to take full advantage of the Tefal Dual Easy Fry & Grill's versatile capabilities. The clear, step-by-step instructions make it accessible for both beginners and experienced cooks alike. It encourages home cooks to experiment with new ingredients and methods, providing plenty of inspiration for expanding their culinary repertoire.

Ultimately, The UK Tefal Dual Easy Fry & Grill Cookbook is more than just a collection of recipes—it's a practical companion that helps you make the most of your Tefal appliance, bringing convenience, variety, and flavour to your kitchen. Enjoy your cooking!

Appendix Recipes Index

Printed in Dunstable, United Kingdom